A Rhapsody of
Words

A RHAPSODY OF WORDS

Ivor Brown

RHAPSODY:
'A collection. A literary work consisting of
miscellaneous or disconnected pieces having no
fixed form or plan.'

RHAPSODICAL:
'Exaggeratedly enthusiastic or ecstatic in
language or manner.'

Oxford English Dictionary

THE BODLEY HEAD

LONDON SYDNEY

TORONTO

© Ivor Brown 1969
SBN 370 00333 0
Printed and Bound in Great Britain for
The Bodley Head Ltd.
9 Bow Street, London WC2
by C. Tinling & Co. Ltd., Prescot
Set in Baskerville Linotype
First published 1969

Foreword

Language, like human beings, can be fat or lean. The idea that obesity and joviality always go together is by no means true. The doctors, as well as fashion, command us to be slim. But in our vocabulary there might still be an occasional welcome for the spread of verbal flesh once admired and now rejected. Such a greetings was given by H. G. Wells's Mr Polly, the draper's assistant who escaped with rapture from his long hours of drudgery into the most flowery fields of literature. He had his own word for rhapsody. 'Sesquippledan', he would say, 'Sesquippledan verboojuice. Eloquent Rapsodooce.' One of his fellow-workers described him as 'In the warehouse, O'Man. All among the tablecloths and blankets. Carlyle. He's reading aloud. Doing the High Froth. Spuming.' He thought language should be a paint-box with plentiful mixing of tints and purple well in mind.

G. K. Chesterton, when he was a Battersea Londoner of the parks and pubs and not yet a sylvan recluse in 'the towns among the beech-woods where men were meant to be', once wrote that the most purple of his hours had been spent on the platforms of Clapham Junction railway station. Few of us are so imaginatively gifted as to find an Eden in that stony Sahara. But a taste for the purple is as natural in fine speech as in fine linen. Few in youth have not been sometimes intoxicated by the alcohol of fermented verboo-juice

5

or fascinated by the dyes of a purple patch in writing. To be so entranced is a proper joy of the young with a flutter in the mind and a pen in hand. For a while they are like the flower-boys and hippies of recent years. In his admirable reflections on life and letters in *The Summing Up* Somerset Maugham reminds us of his rapsodooce years. The confession is astonishing since he later trained himself with the disciplined austerity of an Olympian athlete to write prose of a muscular simplicity with not an ounce of fat on its bones. Few have more rigorously stripped their style of superfluous tissue. But he began as a wallower in a warm bath of words.

He related that he once went to the British Museum to collect rare and rich language for future display. He entered in a note-book the names of strange jewels and sumptuous fabrics. These were to be the treasured elements of writing which would be as rich in texture as a medieval tapestry. He never destroyed them and said that they were lying about somewhere and might be available for 'somebody determined to write nonsense.'

Having visited Spain in his early youth and enjoyed some purple hours in surroundings very different from those which coloured Chesterton's times in Clapham Junction he did write a book called *The Land of the Blessed Virgin* in which, though not a believer, he flung about the flowers of speech. When a reprinting was much later asked for by an American publisher he would not let the text go as it stood. He refused to revise it. That task, he felt, had become intolerable. His juvenile style he found 'wistful, allusive, elaborate' and 'smelling of hot-house plants.' The book was dead. 'It was written,' he decided, 'by one whom I have completely forgotten.'

My own experience has gone the other way. I began with the lean meat. Here I ask pardon for a scrap of youthful autobiography since it explains my later word-hunger and word-fancying which have produced a number of commentaries and anthologies now increased by yet another. A narrowly classical education which produced certain results of scholarship value left me at twenty-two lamentably ignorant of any history and literature which was not Roman or Greek. English literature only came in at the side-door and then briefly.

Some Shakespeare had to be admitted but he was turned into a class-room nuisance. For those set to climb the scholarship ladder he was merely in the way. Greek and Latin took up all my time, offered the main chance and brought in awards. The competition in my school was not formidable. One could pick up a load of books. Even calf-bound volumes of the presentation kind were then cheap. Some of the prizes were of substantial money value and I could choose, within limits, what I liked. This was a precious liberty which made even Swinburne and H. G. Wells permissible. But I went for the Establishment too. Thus without much effort I had acquired by seventeen what the auctioneers call 'A Gentleman's Library'. Since many of its components were in my native language I had no time to read them. Back to the curriculum. On with the ancients. My English reading was minimal, limited to the holidays when there were other attractions.

There was, of course, the English Bible. But religion had been made repellent by compulsory prayers and chapel-going and the dreary load of 'Divinity' lessons. Our Christian instruction was a powerful stimulant of atheism. Why plague boyhood with those savages, the Kings of Israel and Judah, and the itinerary details of St Paul's preaching in Asia Minor? The Acts and the Pauline epistles were read in Greek and without the superb surface of style conferred on all they handled by the Jacobean translators. The Old Testament with all its barbarities can be enjoyed for the new look which they gave it, a fact apparently unknown to my pastors. It never struck the clergymen who took to teaching as well as preaching and were dull dogs at both that the English Bible was a masterpiece and not merely a Set Subject. Hence with small acquaintance of the Elizabethan verboojuice and of the superb adornment of the English language in the following century I had no opportunity to share Mr Polly's delight in the purple patch and the voluptuous roll of syllables. That may have been good discipline. In writing essays one did not froth. But much was being missed.

English is not a language to be wasted. Properly taught it is a stimulant of curiosity and a source of wonder. The excitement of wonder is the essence of good education in any subject literary, historical or scientific. When I went to Oxford at eighteen I was like my fellow sixth-formers, loaded with Greek and Latin. The specialisation was monstrous. I had no modern language except school-boy French. I knew nothing of science and had just enough mathematics to get through. My modern history was a cluster of gaps between periods sketchily covered. Nearly everything was abandoned at fifteen for Extra Classics. I knew of Dr Johnson and Gibbon and the other Big Bow-Wows only as names.

To get a classical scholarship, a necessary rung on the academic ladder, there could be no deviation from ancient past to recent past. The grander use of the English language I had hardly met. The cut and thrust of Tacitus had been familiar. He could kill an Empress in a sentence. 'Messalina tired of adultery because it was so easy.' When Gibbon despatched an imperial scoundrel or crack-pot he did not merely bury him. He conducted the obsequies, as the old-time reporters used to say, with a *cortège* of sentences in noble procession. There was a verbal equipage. His periods were like the mourning plumage of a Victorian funeral. Maugham came to disapprove of Gibbon. He carried his stylistic austerity too far. He was denying one kind of glory. He was wrong. Is the organ-music of our language to be barred?

Thus I did not encounter the 'eloquent rapsodooce' sufficiently to be dazzled and allured by it. There had been a vogue for it at the end of the nineteenth century when Maugham was doing his early reading. The flowers of speech were in fashion and he plucked them for a while. But he soon rebelled, and subsequently confessed his growing aversion to the amplitude of Walter Pater and Ruskin, the recommended exemplars of his youth. After his fascination by Oscar Wilde and the absorption and regurgitation of the linguistic sweets of the nineties he turned from the feast to the fast, deliberately starving himself at the desk in order to produce the utmost directness and lucidity of statement. This he achieved but in the process he seemed to become word-deaf to the sonorities of his own tongue. Yet in the theatre he could applaud the French actors magnoperating without stint in the rhetoric of Racine.

His precept and practice were to use as few adjectives as possible. He liked the sinewy epigram; he hated the lush epithet. He appreciated instrumental music, but he was frightened of the melody and diapason of language.

The fashion in style was going that way, a path with no primroses. My boyhood introduction to good English writing came partly through the plays and prefaces of Bernard Shaw, that paragon of clear and cogent pamphleteering prose. We can say now that he talked some political nonsense—his later acceptance of dictatorships and Police States was shocking—but

9

never in his life was his style pretentious or obscure. His meaning was completely plain to any reader. Much virtue in that. But the excellence of the Fabian essayist produced a body of doctrinal writing with the ribs showing through. He was a highly efficient public speaker but he did not admit the luxury of a Victorian peroration. Some of the politicians did. Lloyd George could revel in a splash of the High Froth. The Welsh, like the Irish, have retained an ear and an appetite for 'the gab'. Churchill knew to perfection when monosyllables were essential in a challenging war-time speech and what could be done with a full vocabulary, especially in writing. What better description of old age than 'the surly advance of decrepitude' with its rumbling, grumbling adjective and its heavy limping noun? The passing of domination from the platform to the microphone and television screen has produced the lingo of the fire-side chat and the calculated cult of the good, plain fellow's image, that fraudulent pest of our time. For the lack of it an able and honest man may be exiled. The look not the language gives the passport to Downing Street and the cathode tube has become the corridor of power. There is no future for the rhythmic elegance of the speaker who gives a civilised polish to the presentment of a policy.

So my chosen models were the controversialists. In that astonishing product, a weekly review called *The New Age* for which the greatest were ready to write for nothing, conflict was briskly conducted by Shaw, G. K. Chesterton, and Hilaire Belloc. The latter couple were linked in the Shavian and Socialist dialectic as a creature called the Chester-Belloc as though they were the partners under the skin of a pantomime-horse. Their creed was inspired by a religious faith not wholly shared since Chesterton had not yet taken the road to Rome. In politics they championed the survival of the peasant proprietor and the independent tradesman and craftsman. They were right in thinking that freedom depends on the right to own. But the world was not going their way. The State nationalised. Big Business became bigger with its take-over bids. But they argued with a passionate conviction and Belloc, High Frothing with his Anglo-French eloquence on a platform, made the words Freedom and Republic, with his rolling 'r's', come crashing like a wave of the sea into a debate with Shaw. That, with the added salt of Shavian wit, could never be dry.

Chesterton, less suited to the dais, made short and ordinary words whirl in a caper of alliteration, pun, and paradox. He had made his name with short newspaper articles in which be excelled. Victorian journalism had been verbose, but Alfred Harmsworth had brought in a vast new public who must not be baffled and deterred by a strange vocabulary. Brevity for the reader in a hurry and common words for the common reader were the Fleet Street rules: Chesterton complied but he gave the short words an exciting twist of his own. His method was magnetic and I was captivated. It was dangerous to the raw imitator. The smartness of school-boys may amuse the authors. It is an affliction to others.

While I read Chesterton I listened to Maugham in the theatre where he had a remarkable success after ten years of neglect. His light comedies had epigrams in plenty, injected, as he later explained, at managerial command. The smart saying was in vogue. Wilde's verboojuice was outdated. His epigrams were not. The aphoristic dialogue demanded a stylish adroitness. The 'crack' which succeeded it did not. But again there was a menace to the aspirant.

Only when released from the Greek and Latin routine could I begin to fill up the enormous gaps in my awareness and enjoyment of English literature. Now I discovered that our language, so variously and richly compounded of the Germanic, Nordic, and Renaissance classicism, was a treasure-chest. Thus Shakespeare, once a plague, became the bringer of delight. Here was language alive and musical, as profuse in melody as in fine shades of meaning. It seemed to me that this wealth had been strangely neglected because the educators had no eyes or ears for strange beauty and simply took the magic for granted. Their Immortal Bard was accepted as the greatest of poets but why that had happened and why the attribution of supremacy was justified they did not inquire. So I began to probe the verbal origins and curious uses of words which particularly pleased, considering the charms of euphony as well as the intricacies of meaning.

Maugham in *The Summing Up* defined the essentials of good writing as lucidity, simplicity and euphony in that order. He had his reasonable dislikes such as a string of 's's'. As a dramatist he had to compose easily speakable dialogue. The lines must be easy on the lips. But for the larger euphony of a full vocabulary he did not care since the narrative style in his novels and short stories is conversational and admits no decoration. The enjoyment of sound in his opinion was for the composer and executant in the concert-hall, not for the author framing a sentence at his desk as it had been in earlier centuries. I do not share his distrust of verbal music or his belief that adjectives are decorative excrescences which always need severe trimming.

I began to make verbal anthologies. That description seemed a fair one. Words which are the material of good writing are flowers just as much as the prose and poems fashioned from them. Why do certain letters of the alphabet or combinations of those letters stir feelings of tranquillity or stimulation, of rapture or repulsion? Why is the impact of some words so powerful when words which are meant to have the same effect are flat and educe no emotion? An obvious example is the lament of Shakespeare's Cleopatra for the loss of Antony.

O withered is the garland of the war.

This with identical meaning could be

O faded is the flower of the fight.

But the first is magical and the second is feeble. In both there is alliteration. But a string of 'f's' is fussy. The interplay of 'r's' and 'w's' has the very genius of mourning and sets the bells tolling. I do not suppose that Shakespeare deliberately altered his flow of speech. The editors of the first Folio, his colleagues who have earned eternal glory by saving and printing his manuscripts, said that he never blotted a line. The superb effects just happened inside this amazing man who was in his great years busily engaged as actor and manager of a repertory company—and no life could be more worrying that that. He did not score out and amend. He was 'a natural'.

To my surprise collecting and commenting on these occurrences created more interest than I had dared to expect. My readers were such eager correspondents that they began to write more Word Books for me. They not only sent me rarities, dialect terms dear to them, and veterans of the vocabulary for whom they wished a revival and rejuvenation. They also let me know of their hates, stupid misusage and the muddled jargon of bureaucracy. They were conscious and resentful of thistles in the flower-beds. Their letters contained a medley of verbal beauties to be fostered, ugliness to be censured and oddities to be collected. So it has gone on and so have I continued to forage and add to the record. That enough is enough we are frequently told. I used to promise that I would do no more, but the provocation continues and the older one becomes the more idle hours one has to fill. To say that convicts me of self-indulgence in plodding on. But it is a harmless ploy and there is one final answer to the writer who becomes a bore, as to the wearisome speaker or television feature on the air. They can be immediately turned off and a book need never be taken up.

A

Ado, Much Of

The termination, not the trouble, is the point of interest because, at the time of writing, I am what some prefer to call incommunicado. Cut off is not for them. One living on the side of a steepish urban hill is impounded by a blizzard with hard frost following. A small mountain range of solid snow separates me from the road which at first was impassable by cars and vans. No postman penetrated. No milkman jangled his cart of bottles. Except for the telephone, which surprisingly did not fail, we were as incommunicado as any prisoner in a Police State cell. This state of affairs may appeal to those who happily hum the refrain of 'Walking in the winter wonderland' and 'I'm dreaming of a white Christmas'. Of such weather I am no afficionado, as the affected fancier of this or that form of art likes to call himself.

But the ado-business has its merits. Wordsworth was aware of that when he added a syllable to barricade and so stressed the pains of

Sorrow barricadoed evermore
Within the walls of cities.

Tornado gains in violence by the thump of its final syllable. The 'immortal passado' mentioned by Mercutio sounds more likely to prove lethal than does a common pass or thrust in fencing. A bastinado is more than a beating. Colorado is the right towering name for a State which has fifty peaks of fourteen thousand feet or more with the rivers and canyons appertaining. Pintado, so useful to makers of cross-word puzzles, has proved a name so attractive to ornithologists that it has become the label of two different types of species, a petrel, also called a Cape Pigeon, and a guinea-fowl.

The boom of the final vowel is equally effective with another letter in front of it.

> Blow winds and crack your cheeks, rage, blow,
> You cataracts and hurricanoes spout.

The tempest in *King Lear* thus thunders in our ears and with its extra syllable out-roars a mere hurricane. So I suppose that to be incommunicado is durance viler that that of mere isolation.

Ambage

We do not now read or hear of an ambagious or ambigatory fellow. (Sir Walter Scott gave the adjective its latter form). The French ambage for equivocation or deceitful ambiguity is described as 'naturalised' in England in the sixteenth century. It is odd that Shakespeare never used it since his appetite for imported words was not less than his power to create new and native ones. It could have fitted in to any of his descriptions of quibbling states-men and intriguing scoundrels. The Porter in *Macbeth* has something to say of equivocation and might have introduced the ambage. He was not only a castle-servant in Scotland's dark ages: his remarks are generally taken to refer to the ambagious Jesuits in the reign of King James the Sixth of Scotland and

First of England. Shakespeare kept to ambiguous and ambiguity which could refer to puzzles as well as dishonest evasion.

> Seal up the mouth of outrage for a while
> Till we can clear these ambiguities

cries Prince Escalus at the end of *Romeo and Juliet*. Hamlet had deceit in mind and the other kind of ambage when he declared his assumption of 'an antic disposition'. That was to be made manifest in meaningless words such as 'There be and if they might' and 'such ambiguous givings out.'

When Dr. Johnson spoke of 'the anfractuosities of the human mind' he was considering intricate deviations of thought and not mental chicanery. Guilt was not implied. Nor could any dishonesty have been suggested by Bacon when he said that life can be prolonged by ambages of diet and bathing. This kind of variation at the table or the tub was blameless and possibly therapeutic. But usually the ambagious politician was an equivocator. The correspondent who once drew my attention to the naturalised French word mentioned 'the tortuous and delaying tactics' of the diplomacy practised in Paris during discussions on Britain's possible entry into the Common Market. Unkind to M. Couve de Murville? If we wish to be courteous it might be more tactful to complain of his intellectual anfractuosities and not of his deliberate ambages.

Autodidact

A review of a life of Ambrose Bierce tells me that he was an autodidact. I should have said that he was self-taught. On the whole I belong to the English

17

Speaking Union, not the Anglo-Hellenists. Because I had an exclusively classical education, I had to find out for myself what had happened in my own country and what was written in my own language. This involved a process which some would call post-graduate autodidacticism. There are lamentable gaps in my knowledge. Were I examined on English history up to 1483 and especially on the causes, events, and personalities of the Wars of the Roses I should be well below the O-level. This is not so deplorable as it sounds since I find the Anglo-Saxon period dreary and deterrent and the ruins of Norman castles monotonous and tedious. What arts did their marauding owners possess? The Church knew about beauty. The great cathedrals were going up, miraculous achievements of anonymous men. Outside them other persons unknown were writing and acting the Mystery Plays. There was a richness which the badly written history primers of my schooling forgot to mention. Then came Chaucer, too difficult in language, and too naughty in his narrative, for the curriculum of the period. The classroom history books were mainly populated by royal and baronial thugs. When the Elizabethan glory came to the English language I was not informed of it and had to discover it for myself.

The temptation to display one's acquaintance with those languages which are called dead but are continually revived in the vocabulary of the sciences is evidently strong. Aldous Huxley was much inclined that way. A broad-bottomed character he called eurypygous. If he had written about Ambrose Bierce he might have called him autoptic since Bierce used his eyes in close and rewarding personal observation when a soldier in the American Civil War. (It is curious that autopsy should now be limited to the medical inspection of a corpse. The conductors of

18

autopsies are not investigating the causes of their own demise. Necropsy is the correct term.) Those recording the Ministerial career of Mrs Barbara Castle could at one time have called her the autocratrix of the transport world. That was a title applied to a wilful Empress of Russia, Catherine the Second. People delighting in such displays of erudition are unlikely to be autodidacts themselves. I believe that the indefatigable Dame Sybil Thorndike taught herself ancient Greek. But most scholars have had schooling or tuition.

It is now, I suppose, pedantic to cavil at words in which Greek and Latin are mixed. Those who do complain must shudder if invited to lunch at the Royal Automobile Club by one who is also a member of the Automobile Association. Autokinetic would suit them better. The first enthusiasts for self-moving vehicles were not purists when they called upon the ancient world to describe the inventions of the new. But when a word of mixed origins has become established it has to be accepted. Who is going to insist on teleoptics instead of television?

Just after this was written Mr Richard Marsh, Mrs Castle's successor at the Ministry of Transport, said in her praise that 'she could make the word containerisation sound like a quatrain from Omar Khayyam.' It would be a melodious world in which our politicians and technologists used the rhythms and vocabulary of Edward Fitzgerald.

Azalea

A friend has thanked me for the gift of an azalea and has set me wondering why the flower ever got

19

that name. Some easy research tells me that it is derived from the Greek for dry. A plant without a thirst it can 'bloom profusely in sandy soil'. Yet British gardeners do not find that it needs a desert. It seems to grow well enough in clay. It has reached us from far and wide, America, Japan, and the Caucasus. It does not appear to be 'choosy' in its new homes.

Shakespeare made zed a term of contempt and abuse. In *King Lear* the worthy Kent, who has showed his ownership of a comprehensive vocabulary of vituperation in his dealings with Goneril's steward Oswald, rails at him 'Thou whoreson zed! Thou unnecessary letter!' Whether or not we require the last letter in the alphabet it is harsh to the ear. There is a certain charm in the roll of consonants in Azalea, but the zed has ruined its chance of becoming a Christian name. I cannot remember hearing of a girl called Azalea. Contracted to Azzie it would be hideous. I know of a genial Oswald who is Ozzie to his friends, but that is an unworthy noise unfair to the man in question.

Azalea is now less than ever likely to be heard at a christening ceremony since flower-names are far out of fashion. Even the best of them, the simple and beautiful rose, is a rarity. There was a time, associated in my memory with *Punch* in A. A. Milne's day, when there were Dahlias in the humorist's garden. Some women of that name were, I suppose, to be met in the charming person. But Dahlia, which ought to have a broad 'a' being named after Herr Dahl, a Swedish botanist, has vanished from the christening font and so have the Violets. Now we are all for plain, traditional monosyllables. The Annes and Janes have driven the Lilies off the field. For Azalea there is small hope and, if one were to appear, she might be expected by a student of dictionaries to be a very dry party and to refuse her coffee in mid morning and her stronger liquors later in the day. There is an adjective anti-Bacchic which would seem suitable to the unbibulous Azalean girl. But that is a term for a metrical foot containing two long syllables and one short and is not relevant to abstainers from liquidity.

Aziola

To a famous poet the word Aziola was at first forbidding. A monstrous feminine bore loomed up before his flinching eyes. But he was relieved of the menace. He even became enraptured.

'Do you not hear the Aziola cry?
Methinks she must be nigh,'
    Said Mary, as we sate
In dusk, ere stars were lit, or candles brought;
    And I, who thought
This Aziola was some tedious woman,
Asked, 'Who is Aziola?' how elate
I felt to know that it was nothing human,
No mockery of myself to fear or hate:
    And Mary saw my soul,
And laugh'd, and said, 'Disquiet yourself not;
    'Tis nothing but a little downy owl.'

Sad Aziola! many an eventide
    Thy music I had heard
By wood and stream, meadow and mountain side,
And fields and marshes wide,
Such as nor voice, nor lute, nor wind, nor bird,
    The soul ever stirr'd;
Unlike, and far sweeter than them all.

21

Sad Aziola! from that moment I
Loved thee and thy sad cry.

The author is Shelley. The lines are not, I think,
familiar.

B

Bats in the Belfry

The description of dementia has had a plentiful
ration of slang. Dotty and potty were commonly used
and now are rarely used. They are dull and feeble
terms. Cracked originally meant bankrupt in money
before it meant bankrupt in mind. It has had
crackers and crackpot as variants. Mental deviation has
provided its forms of curvature such as loopy and
round the bend. But a person now described as bent
is crooked in conduct not adrift in his mind. Bonkers,
which Eric Partridge notes as naval slang for slightly
drunk or light-headed in 1920, has been lately promoted in the verbal crazy gang and now appears to
mean wholly daft. There is a vogue for nuts and
nutty. A nut, sometimes spelled with a 'k', had been
a dandy. He is now in the bonkers class, but the
word is a paltry one.

Bats and batty are shortened forms of Bats in the
Belfry. This last is an astonishing piece of imagery
and its unknown creator brought a touch of genius
into slang. The vision of the brain as a dark and

lonely tower in which the flitter-mice are circling is so far from being a joke as to be terrifying. To call the bat a repellent fly-by-night is to put it mildly. The feminine horror of getting one of these vespertilians enmeshed in the human hair is natural. Modern hair-styles may bring many young men also into that embarrassment. A bat on the top of the head is bad enough. A bat within it is a more loathsome thought.

G. K. Chesterton said that slang is the poetry of the people. So it can be, but in fact much of it is prose of an unimaginative kind. But the linking of the sweeping bats with the gloom and solitude of a steeple's lofty cavern was the work of one who was indeed a poet, worthy of high ranking in the sombre and macabre school. It sets one thinking of the maniacs in the Elizabethan and Jacobean plays. It is good enough for John Webster, that master of the ghoulish vision and the line that shrieks like a mandrake. His Duchess of Malfi, tormented by a parade of lunatics, might have fainted with bats and belfries on her lips. Being now familiar the phrase could rouse a laugh among some members of the audience. But it deserves not a giggle but a shudder. It is more sinister than 'bees in the bonnet'. If the bees are swarming that is certainly a fearsome simile, but to regard the brain as a bonnet is not so terrifying as to think of it as a dark bat-haunted tower.

Beauty

I noticed in an article on modern slang in the *Daily Mail* that the words expressing feminine rapture have worn themselves out. The smashing, the fabulous, the too divine, the super-duper are 'out'. The young, we were told, had returned to the simplicity of 'Beautiful'. They might do worse. Certainly 'fab' has been worked to death.

Seeing that Norman Douglas's *South Wind* was fifty years old I revisited as a reader his Sirocco-sweltering island of Nepenthe as much for the Mediterranean climate of his sun-baked prose as for his Capri characters. (There is not much doubt about the scene of the book's occasionally dramatic events and continual fecundity in conversation.) A charming talker is Count Caloveglia: I found his discussions with the yachting American millionaire van Koppen well worth re-reading. They argued about beauty. Could a machine, though well-designed and functioning perfectly, be given the same attribute as the sculpture of Praxiteles? The American thought that it could. He had the ideal motor-car in mind. The Count protested that a work of art has the mystery of eternal youth whereas the best of machines, the consummately efficient and smooth-running engine, while having an excellence of its own, grows obsolete and ends on the scrap-heap. Our language, he decided, is sadly inadequate for the description of assorted beauties. 'This', he thought, 'should make us careful as to the words we employ and ready to coin new ones when a new idea is expressed. If we enlarge our concepts, we should likewise enlarge our vocabulary.'

Unfortunately he did not add any practical suggestion to this reasonable counsel. How do we expand our language to describe our various notions of the beautiful? The words at our command are few enough. Beauty has been tossed about in every direction, from the looks of a human face to a move in a field of play. 'What a beauty!' is exclaimed by the spectator of batsmanship in cricket or of a long approach to the green in golf as well as by the entranced admirers of a motor-car faultless in looks,

24

comfort, and speed. Incidentally both Douglas's talkers would have agreed on the potential beauty of bold and ingenious mendacity. They were great liars in practice and respected expertise in false pretences. The 'whopper' in slang could have been a beauty to them if it were craftily and convincingly made. Beauty has become an all-purpose word as its present appearance in juvenile slang reveals. I myself had not heard it so employed when I read about it, but the journalist obviously knew her subject.

It occurs to me that van Koppen's raptures over his Cadillac car and similar triumphs of engineering might have been better expressed with the use of an old English word now rarely used. That is our form of the Latin adjective *concinnatus* which has provided our noun concinnity defined as 'skilful fitting together of parts, harmony'. Concinnity therefore could apply as much to a musical composition or a theatrical production as to a piece of skilfully contrived machinery. It has slipped out of our vocabulary and, if now used, might be found puzzling and thought affected. That raises the vexing problem of expanding our language by revival of things forgotten. Writers do not want to annoy their readers by recourse to words now unknown or invented. Yet, if we never draw on the past or devise a novelty, the English language becomes wretchedly constricted.

Comely is now almost an antique. To call a person comely, says Oxford, 'implies a homelier style of beauty, which pleases without exciting admiration'. To call a girl homely in American is so far from flattering her looks as to be almost rude. I myself would not be deterred by a caterer who offered 'good homely fare', but the gourmet journalists who commend *haute cuisine* at their commended establishments would regard homely feeding as barbarous. Milton, who used homely in the disparaging way preserved across the ocean, did not disdain comeliness. It is pleasantly linked—one might say with concinnity of phrasing—in 'Il Penseroso' where civil-suited Morn appears (with the original spelling) as

Chercheft in a comly Cloud
While rocking Winds are Piping loud.

Shakespeare associated comely more with proper conduct than with pleasing looks. For him 'comely love' was linked with sincerity. Happier times were also comely. Virtue too was given that adjective.

When Keats wrote

Beauty is truth, truth beauty—That is all
Ye know on earth, and all ye need to know,

he was not saying anything with a clear meaning. That is well enough if you think that poets need not make lucid judgments. Meaningful is an adjective which I avoid, but it is dear to some seekers after the Highest Thinking. Is there any meaning in linking verity and good looks? Many truthful statements are ugly and harsh while falsehoods are bland and may be beautiful. Truth may be necessary but it does not charm. Beauty, like truth, is as hard to define as it is to discover in a jarring and squalid world. But it may be generally agreed that Norman Douglas's Count had a point. We need more words for it.

Besom

In our permissive age there are strange impermissible practices. One is to call an old person old in an official statement or document. I am, as Yorkshire folk say, 'living on borrowed time' but I can see no shame in that condition. 'Advancing years' are a burden, not a disgrace. Public authorities may shiver at the word old, but public speech admits it and quite rudely too. A bureaucrat may arrange gerontological therapy for a Senior Citizen (Female). But in the street or the bar-parlour you may hear her called an Old Bag.

Once she would have been an Old Besom with some unkindly adjective attached. That word was also used as a verb. Besom does not suggest a house-proud and scrupulously cleanly old lady. But, if she did happen to do some sweeping, she could be said to besom her room since a besom was a broom before it became an elderly woman. The indication was usually of unsightly aspect and surly temper. It seems to me likely that besom was a name used through association with a witch's broomstick. That idea is supported by the origin of the word hag which was the Old English *haga* meaning a bush. It was supposed that witches lurked in the hedges and undergrowth. There is the further oddity that an old besom, bag, or hag has long been called an old faggot. A faggot, like some kinds of broom, was a bundle of sticks. A witch who rode on a broom had both a single stick and a collection of twigs below her. She was doubly a besom.

Shakespeare used that word once as a broom. 'I am the besom that must sweep the Court clean of such filth as thou art', he makes Jake Cade shout at Lord Say (*Henry VI, Part 2, Act IV, Scene 7*). But he never called an old woman a besom or a faggot. The Weird Sisters in *Macbeth* gave him a chance, but they are described as hags of a 'secret, black, and midnight' kind. He said nothing of a harridan. That is explained as an English word for a jaded and worthless horse.

James Thurber wrote an admirable commentary

on the way in which the English have libelled their favourite animals. Dogs are beloved, but the name is contemptuous when applied to mankind. There are pups, who are insolent, curs who are despicable, and bitches who are lewd and malicious. Shakespeare made spaniel a contemptuous verb for to fawn and grovel. The horse is deemed a noble animal but to call an author a hack, or a Senior Citizen (Female) a harridan or jade is to show the utmost discourtesy to the stable. To speak of a young man as a stallion would be a compliment to his virility but not a description generally acceptable. But I wander from the broomsticks! An unpopular old woman, if there must be abusive language, might well prefer old besom to old bag when the taunts are in the air.

Blab

Blab, both verb and noun for the garrulous types, and especially for those who through indiscretion or treachery betray a friend, had a place in poetry before it sank to be slang or something near it. Shakespeare wrote 'Beaufort's red sparkling eyes blab his heart's malice'. The Captain in *Twelfth Night* promises that his lips will not blab Viola's disguise as a boy. Milton introduced blab into the exalted language of *Samson Agonistes*. Says the tragic hero

How heinous had that been, how deserving
Contempt and scorn of all, to be excluded
All friendship and avoided as a blab.

The blab became a sneak in schoolboy talk. The villains frequently met and cornered in such television series as *Zed Cars* and *Softly, Softly* are not victims of blabbing when an old colleague in crime gives them away. They are grassed. Partridge dates the first use of grassing as 1933. Presumably it came from the football field. A player fairly tackled in Rugby football or unfairly tripped up in the Association game is grassed.

Returning to the Shakespearian blab I find myself bewildered by the extremely curious lines spoken by the Captain of a ship in the Second Part of *Henry VI* (*Act IV, Scene I*). The stage-hands had been busily engaged in the contrivance of 'Alarum. Fight at sea. Ordnance goes off. Enter a Captain, Master, and Master's Mate, and others with prisoners, including the Duke of Suffolk'. The Captain, who evidently in the nautical ranking of the time was superior to a Master, has a rich vocabulary and thus explains the capture and demands money down, a ransom of two thousand crowns. The episode is rich in rhetoric. The Captain sets the scene by beginning thus,

> The gaudy, blabbing, and remorseful day
> Is crept into the bosom of the sea,
> And now loud-roaring wolves arouse the jades
> That drag the tragic, melancholy night;
> Who, with their drowsy, slow, and flagging wings
> Clip dead men's graves and from their misty jaws
> Breathe foul contagious darkness on the eve.

Here is fine mixed verbal feeding and a grand opportunity for minor actors to 'bombast'. But what are those horses who make nocturnal flights like owls? Why is the day called blabbing? The other epithets can be explained. The day has been gaudy with a battle which lasted till sunset. Remorseful can be a transferred adjective indicating the chagrin of the humiliated Duke and his companions in defeat. But how did the day blab? Was there a misprint with blub in the manuscript? The defeated had cause

29

for tears and Shakespeare used blubber, if not blub, for crying. Juliet's Nurse describes the girl's blubbering. It is a puzzle and it is no less so if it be claimed that this is a contribution by Marlowe or another to this possibly composite play. But we must not grumble. The lines make a wonderful noise and had an audience which relished not only Ordnance going off at sea but waves of bombast roaring in. If the imagery were a bit muddled what cared they? They had their verbal music fortissimo.

Blob

When a batsman fails to score at cricket we are now told by the television commentators that he has 'failed to get off the mark'. When I was a cricketer there was none of that polite dismissal of my incompetence. I had made a blob, a performance all too frequent. A blob or bleb might also be a glob since it is 'a pimple or globule of liquid or viscous substance', a nasty eruption, especially if visible. The artist in gouache might be called a blobber since he uses globulous material, 'opaque colours ground in water and mixed with gum and honey'. Having seen the achievements in gouache of Mr J. B. Priestley I rank him as a most gifted blobber.

I was set thinking about blobs by an article in the Journal of the Lancashire Dialect Society whose industrious members had been doing some valuable word-research among the sea-fishing communities in many of our ports. The jelly-fish is so repulsive and sometimes so dangerous a creature that it has naturally evoked a number of deterrent names. In Cumberland this flabby scion of the family of *Scopelidæ* is called a slob, in Yorkshire a blob or blobby-lumper and a laverack, in Devon a blubber, in Kent a slutter, in Lincolnshire a slunder, and a lammoo in the Isle of Man. The stinging species are snodgorls at Harwich, and cow-kites at Fleetwood. Elsewhere they are ju-jus, Portuguese warships, and, if vast, cabbage-blobs. The bather on our coasts who finds the sea blob-infested has a large vocabulary of disgust from which to choose. I find blobby-lumper most satisfactory. Since lumper is also a verb meaning to move clumsily and blunder along I have too often been a blobby-lumper when handling a bat at the wicket.

Boggle

This is one of the verbs which have become associated with a single noun. 'The mind boggles at the thought.' Because of the sticky bog on the moors or on marshland one thinks of a mind that has become stuck in the mud of confusion and is therefore immobile, fumbling and bungling.

That is all wrong. A boggling mind should be jumping hither and thither. To boggle was to dart away in fear like a startled animal. It shares its roots with the bogey, bogle, or boggart who made human beings go boggling into swift, evasive action.

The King in *All's Well That Ends Well* says that Bertram, who has been dodging marriage, boggles when he is cornered. When Antony, enraged with Cleopatra, cries 'You were a boggler ever' and enumerates her 'hotter hours' he is not calling her a fool. Far from it. He is describing her nimble changes of course, half passionate and half political, among her Roman lovers.

The original meaning of boggle has gone. The

supreme footballers who are masters of the swerving or jinking run would not thank a reporter who, knowing his Shakespeare, described them as bogglers. That to the modern reader would imply a missed chance of scoring, and the opposite of agility.

Bomb

How does one keep up with theatrical jargon? Playhouse 'bombs' are exploding round me, sometimes indicating a crash of applause and sometimes a destructive disdain. First I learn from a London paper that Ena Sharples, the Tanners, and the other regulars of Granada Television's veteran favourite *Coronation Street* are 'going a bomb' in Hong Kong where, with Cantonese dubbing, the series is making the Chinese crowd in ecstasy round their screens. That East and West can never meet except in conflict is a view shattered by our Ena, who may be deemed a formidable bombardier if that kind of missile is a symbol of triumph.

An hour later I read some American news which told me that 'New Haven is not only the home of Yale University but also the scene of many pre-Broadway bombs'. This means that plays tried out before entering costly and hazardous New York frequently fail to satisfy their audiences and promoters. In that case they are said to have bombed on the way. Audacious therefore was the dramatist who called his anti-war play 'We Bombed in New Haven'. I write without knowing its fate. The detonation may, if all went well, have been a soaring rocket of success. But often there are sad and expensive explosions of hopes and efforts.

In Britain plays may be hits or flops instead of being more excitingly blown up for good or ill. We are altogether less dramatic in our vocabulary of disappointment and disaster. Students continue to fail in their exams whereas in America they flunk them. We have the odious verb to boob for making a mess of things and I would rather be told that a book of mine had bombed than that it had boobed. It is uncommon to say here that a play disliked and abandoned has laid an egg. But we continue to use love and duck for an absence of points at lawn-tennis and for a total failure at cricket. It is odd that love and duck, like theatrical bombs, should have such various and contrasted meanings. Both express personal affection. Yet both denote failure in a game. It is curious also that the adjective ovate means egg-shaped and therefore suggests negation and inability to score while an ovation is a burst of applause evoked by a brilliant performance. The latter word is a mistake. It should be an avation, if true to its Latin origin. Ave is a cry of welcome.

The menacing word bomb had an innocent start, as the Spanish bomba, a humming noise. It passed from the bees to the bombardiers and since then has increasingly created havoc instead of honey. It also gave the musician the powerful brass of the bombardon. The smaller of God's creatures come into it again with the formidable bombasine of Victorian ladies which owed its sonorous title to the Greek name for a silk-worm. Bombast, now usually confined to noisy, pretentious, and blustering speech, has the same textile origin as bombasine. It was the padding of the prolix orator. When we get to bombus we are back with the buzzers. It is 'a humming noise in the intestines, ears etc.' There is a bombus of boredom or distressful unrest in the minds or entrails of an audience when a play bombs in the West while Miss

Sharples is making her peaceful and admired bombing-raid on the 'goggle-boxes' of Hong Kong.

Brosher

The copy-writers of Travel and Holiday Brochures, broshers to many of their readers, live a busy life and a hard one. The advertising of pleasure beaches and of 'sun-spots' where apparently no cloud is ever seen appears in mass immediately after Christmas and the mass seems vastly to increase its beckoning blend of prose and pictures every year. The composers of the English which I think of as brosher prose are active but inevitably frustrated. Is there anything new to be said? If I were one of their number and wanted to brush up my brosher and give it a new lustre I should be much perplexed. The air of which they tell is inevitably fresh. How fresh can their language be?

It is essential that the reader should not be puzzled. The words used must be familiar. Dream, long used as an adjective, has not yet faded out. Those who have been sold 'a dream home' must have dream escapes from it. The beaches continue to be golden (Shakespeare's yellow sands would sound a bit drab by brosher standards) and the views are always breath-taking. If there is a 'majesty of encircling hills', described as magnetic to the pedestrian, the possible loss of breath and palpitations of the heart which may beset the holiday walker of middle age are not to be thought of. To the brosherist we are all young and swinging.

Those commissioned to sell a resort have sometimes to give simultaneous praise to its peaceful, old-world atmosphere and its new-world pleasures which hardly suggest tranquillity. I read of one Mediterranean paradise which is commended as 'unspoilt'. Yet we are told that it offers buses and motor-launches hurtling at all hours to neighbouring Edens. It has 'numerous friendly bars', 'an attractive night-club with floor-shows and dancing till four in the morning', and 'a ten-pin bowling alley'. Complete absence of spoliation seems doubtful.

However, one cannot blame the copy-writer. The paradise, whose owners employ the advertising agency which employs him, must have something for all tastes. Doubtless it has a niche where not a guitar is to be heard, where nobody rolls a bowl, and where there is one bar for those who like to have a drink without a juke-box, and where it is possible to dodge the amicability promised. It is not only the sour misanthrope who shrinks from comradeship without stint.

The brosherists are not forbidden to use any long words. Some of these have become acceptable to those seeking a hilarious and sun-drenched fortnight. A resort is enhanced by a claim to be sophisticated which one takes to be much the same as permissive. Exotic is a popular adjective. The 'boutique with a rich store of novelties' and 'a maze of quaint old curiosity shops' may be featured as attractions. But the antiquarianism must be kept out of the prose. An ingenious and well-paid writer broshering to earn a holiday of his own would naturally like to enlarge his vocabulary.

A recruit to the profession who knows his poets might yearn to call a landscape with a charming variety of colour daedal, the glassy waters of a quiet creek hyaline instead of crystal-clear, and an Ionian sea-scape at sunset wine-dark or hyacinthine. If he yielded to such temptation he would lose his job.

35

Those drawn to the Balearic shores or isles of Greece by news of all-night 'frugging' and ten-pin bowling alleys are not to be baffled by 'gab' of that kind. The coloured photography must do the work and abundantly does it. Were there ever such blues as the broshering camera-man can produce?

However I have just noted one stranger unexpected in the catalogue of words that spell (and sell) delight. I am invited to take a Harlequin Holiday. That suggests a daedal spangle and a coat of many colours in which to practise all the graces of agility. Many would like to caper with Columbine in a resort which is both sophisticated and unspoilt, is 'out of this world' and has 'much English spoken', and whose hotels supply a rich variety of local dishes, 'chips with everything', and a 'friendly house-party atmosphere'. On then to the Harlequinade. Unfortunately some of us, myself included, have creaking joints and limbs incapable of a swinger's pirouette. I more resemble decrepit Pantaloon for whose stiff shanks the broshers do not cater.

Buffer

We think of buffers only as seniors, substantial members of the fogey and codger class. The fribble is a light-weight and when I read in an American story of 'an old pappy guy' I visualise physical as well as mental frailty. Buffers in the railway station are solid and solid one imagines them in human form.

In personal description old is an adjective inseparable from buffers. Why must they be ancients? O.E.D. defines them simply as foolish fellows and says nothing of their years. Since juvenile fools are as common as senile fools there can surely be young buffers. There is a curiosity here. We are always hearing of old fools and young fools, never of middle-aged fools. Do forty years certainly guarantee sagacity?

The buffer, an ass at any age, could be a buffle-head in the seventeenth century. That epoch had a large vocabulary of contempt for the dolt. It liked a thick stick to cudgel thick heads. We prefer such meagre monosyllables as clot and nut. Nut supposes a mind deranged as well as feeble. In the past language of some bulk was preferred. Along with the buffle-heads were the clod-pates, dunder-pates, and jobbernowls. Niffle was another word of less impact but aptly derisive of the paltry types at whom the superior sniff. 'A rout of niffles', wrote an Elizabethan dramatist of the audience which had failed to appreciate his comedy. Niffle does not bring to mind the weighty block-head who is a buffer. It suits the slender fribble. Aguecheek was not called a niffle but behaved as one. Now he would be called a nit-wit and that is a poor little term for the kind of character to whom our ancestors gave some thumping names.

C

Caligulism

Horace Walpole used this word to describe one who practised the peculiarities for which the fourth Roman

Emperor was infamous. Some of these were jests, some savageries. This homicidal lunatic had a grim sense of humour. When a number of his subjects were watching the barbarities and slaughters in the Colosseum he decided that the penalty of such callousness should fit the crime. So he had the spectators thrown to the lions. He gave a banquet for guzzlers on a bridge of boats and had them thrown overboard to take the waters. That he chose his horse to be his fellow Consul indicates an attitude to political bigwigs which many of his subjects may have shared. Caligula was a murderous scoundrel who watched executions while eating his meals.

But at least one of his capers was bloodless. He marched his legions to the Channel coast for a new invasion of Britain. Then he thought better of that risky undertaking and ordered his troops to collect the sea-shells and take them home as the spoils of a war that never happened. There were four years of imperial Caligulism. After this he was himself despatched by members of the Praetorian Guard. His real name was Gaius Caesar and he got his nick-name from his fondness for the *caliga* or military boot. He thus was the first of the jackboot maniacs who could be rightly called Caligulists.

Caraway

A slice of seed-cake with a glass of sherry or madeira was once a favourite form of 'elevenses' in comfortable English homes. With less leisure and less money we make coffee, probably of the kind known as instant, with a companion biscuit, take the place of the rich Victorian refreshment at mid-day. I like the sound of caraway, vaguely bringing to mind the enchanting sound of faraway, though the 'a' is not a broad one for us. It offers agreeable suggestions of trouble dispelled and of an engine which does not stall. Also I happen to like the flavour of the seed.

Mr Justice Shallow invited Falstaff to his Cotswold orchard to 'eat a last year's pippin of my own graffing, with a dish of caraways and so forth'. Seeds and pippins were also associated with ancestral cooking, the baked apple being served with caraway sauce, a custom which I gather is kept up in some ancient foundations. To some palates caraways are utterly repulsive, but they had a powerful champion in the Baroness Lehzen, Queen Victoria's able and imperious governess and later her rather troublesome companion. Lytton Strachey related of Lehzen that 'her passion for them (caraway seeds) was uncontrollable'. She had special consignments sent from Germany and sprinkled them on all her food from bread and butter to roast beef. Always she carried them about as an alcoholic secretes little bottles in case of desperate need. If, as probable, the Hanoverian potentate of young Vicky's school-room pronounced the word as a caravay it is not less pleasant to the ear. When the ladies of the Court made a jest of the seedy addiction the Baroness was not amused. Whether she abandoned her indulgence is not explained by the biographer.

Casualty

While the slaughter in Vietnam was reaching its most horrible forms and dimensions I noticed that the Americans rarely used the evasive word casualty to which we have been made accustomed in our own wars. They frankly spoke of killed and wounded. A casualty is defined as 'a chance occurrence'. There is no reason, apart from habit, why it should not be used of a happy event. Yet nobody describes a win in a lottery or a successful venture in gambling as a casualty. Since the word is now always applied to bad and bloody news it could be fairly applied to the victims of a railway accident or a crash on the road. There may have been carelessness or recklessness in either case but nobody was intending to cause loss of life.

War too has its accidents but most of the so-called casualties are the result of deliberate killing and maiming. Massacre is the object of the exercise. To say that 'immense casualties were inflicted on the enemy' and that 'our casualties were slight' is nonsensical if we keep to the proper meaning of the term. But those who issue such bulletins are too squeamish to say what was intended and achieved. This is dishonest and the American candour is commendable. Killing is not less repulsive if wrapped in verbal cotton-wool. To use an escape word in this connection is to practise what the moral philosophers call Casuistry whose meaning is 'that part of ethics which resolves cases of conscience and is often applied to a quibbling or evasive way of dealing with difficult cases of duty'. It is also defined as 'sophistry'. The soldier's duty is primarily homicidal. Who talks of casualties in war is a casuist.

Charismatic

I have noticed in the articles of Mr David Wood, a political correspondent of *The Times,* the use of the adjective charismatic when he is discussing the qualities of certain statesmen whose manœuvres he surveys. I gathered from the context that he was alluding to their power to charm the House of Commons and the electors with spell-binding powers.

Charm has come to us from the Latin carmen and began its life as a song. The song pleased and developed a magical influence. It cast the required spell. The Top-pop Singers with their hysterical and screaming 'fans' are charmers in their own way.

Later came the lighter, personal, and usually feminine charm of which Sir James Barrie wrote in his political comedy 'What Every Woman Knows'. The star performers of Harley Street, when the highest rank of medical practice was more fashionable and commercial that it is now, charmed with their bedside manner. It was said of one of the most eminent that his charm always made the relatives feel that the patient could not have died in better hands. The politician's charm persuades us that the affairs of the nation could not be mismanaged with a more devoted integrity of purpose. We hear his smooth and ready words and watch the simple sincerity so impressively presented on the television screen. The charismatic performer at Westminster has the skilled actor's ability to make a string of words effective beyond their merits.

Charisma, however, has no verbal connection with carmen or charm. My two-volume edition of the Oxford English Dictionary spells it Charism with no final 'a'. This, some may think, brings the service-able swabbings and scrubbings of Mrs Mopp into the picture. The definition of Charism exalts it to celestial heights. It is 'a favour specially vouchsafed by God; a grace or talent'. A heaven-sent gift is the essence of the word derived from the Greek Charis, the grace of spirit whose work is charity in the widest sense.

Oxford did not admit the adjective charismatic. If it had done so it would have credited with a divine inspiration the politician who is so described when he is adroitly slipping out of trouble. Professor Garmondsway and his associate in the new Penguin English Dictionary leave the deity out of it. To them charisma is 'a spiritual gift; an extraordinarily high degree of artistic genius'. So, if a statesman is charismatic he is one with Shakespeare, Beethoven, and Rembrandt. He is denied divine afflatus, but as a man of our world he could hardly ask for loftier promotion.

Clobber

This has become a vogue word for practice of assault and battery. When some defenceless old woman who keeps a small shop is attacked by the all too common gangs of till-robbing ruffians she is described in the reports of the crime as having been clobbered. There is an extension of the verb to verbal attack in the angry disputations of our time. A Minister who has been fiercely assailed in Parliament is said to have been clobbered. There are complaints that those who choose to be interviewed in radio and television programmes are cruelly clobbered by inquisitorial conductors of these features. The victims should have known, when they accepted the invitation to appear on the screen and presumably expected to profit by the publicity, that clobbering might ensue. At least such battery breaks no bones and since the sufferer gets paid for his share in what the Scots call a tulzie or stramash his till is not rifled but filled. Furthermore he is not a conscript but volunteers for

42

the possible punishment. I have just read of a boxing champion who was described as clobbered, not by a rival. The knock-out came from the tax-gatherer.

Clobber is, I suppose, one of the collision words, clubbing having been telescoped with robbing. It has not yet made its way into the dictionaries with this meaning. I discover that Dickens used it as a noun meaning 'a black paste used by cobblers to fill up and conceal cracks in leather'. The old clobber which mended shoes is a long way from the new clobbering which breaks heads in the street, reputations on the air, and floors a man with a tax-demand of monstrous size.

Clout for a blow or a bash has been temporarily ousted by clobber. That has partly lost its place in the vocabulary of our apparel, but clobber, meaning clothes in general, survives in slang. The clout as a form of clothing is an antique, at least in the South of England. It lingers in the proverbial warning against casting a clout 'ere May be out', which has been proved sensible advice in recent years in Britain when 'the darling buds of May' were being clobbered by winds as icy as they were rough. The precise meaning of this admonition is disputed. Are we to retain winter under-wear until the first of June or only until the May trees are in blossom? I cannot answer that query but I like to hear in the North of England that clouts are still clothes as well as clobberings.

In that retention the North is being Biblical. The prophet Jeremiah was hauled up from his dungeon by Ebed-Melech the Ethiopian who brought with him 'old cast clouts and old rotten rags' to put under his arm-holes before the hoist. They do not suggest security in a lifting operation, but they served. 'So they drew up Jeremiah.' The rotten rags would offer little safety but the clouts which provided his cords

must have been cast before they decayed. Clouts
have vanished from the southern wardrobe and are
less frequent in the language of lambasting. The
ancient form of that was lamback which suggests
posterior chastisement. The clobberers, going mainly
for the top and not the bottom of their victims, now
hold the ring. In Scotland the violent castigators
have long skelped the objects of their anger and I
think they still do among the Mrs McClobbers of the
wynds and tenements.

Coddle

Sir Thomas Overbury who wrote acute studies of
Elizabethan and Jacobean Characters mentioned one
who had been 'taken from grammar-school half-
coddled'. He did not mean that the boy had been
somewhat petted and half spoiled. To coddle then
was to cook; his education had warmed him up,
perhaps, but left him a bit raw. We retain the kitchen
imagery in our talk of one half-baked. Coddle meaning
fuss over was a nineteenth-century usage. Before that
it was an oven-side word. 'We'll go', wrote Sterne,
'while dinner is coddling.' It was probably a slurred
form of caudle, 'a hot drink of thin gruel mixed with
wine or ale, sweetened and spiced'. This does not
suggest a eupeptic concoction, however agreeable to
the palate. But it was given to invalids. That explains
why coddle changed its meaning from cooking to
cosseting. Cosset began its life as a noun. It was a
motherless or deserted lamb reared by kindly human
hands and presumably bottle-fed.

'Those who wanted to save money on housing a
pig put him under a thatch of the woody stems of

the Coddle-Apple, a local name for the Great Hairy Willow-herb which grows up to six feet high along the ditches.' This from a book by Mr R. E. Moreau about life in an Oxfordshire village with the enchanting name of Berrick Salome at the beginning of the century. Delightful too were some of the names there given to the Coddle-Apple, Blooming Sally, Custard Cups, Fiddle Grass and Son-before-the-Father. It was also Apple Pie, Cherry Pie, Sod Apple (Sodden apple) and other puddingy titles. The last of these are explained by the fruity smell of the willow-herb which spreads easily on all sorts of ground as Londoners discovered on the bomb-sites after the war. It needs no horticultural cosseting.

The codling was a hard or half-grown apple not fit to be eaten raw. Malvolio described Viola, halfway between man and boy, 'as a squash before it is a peascod or a codling when it is almost an apple'. The immature apples, stewed or coddled in the old sense, were sold on the streets of London and gave the great clown Grimaldi the subject of a song 'Hot Codlins' which became one of his most popular 'numbers'.

Colocynth

Kipling said of the English flowers that they sang themselves into poetry. If it be argued that poetry is not achieved by name-dropping, however charming the names, it is hardly deniable that the elements of pleasant-sounding verse abound in our gardens and hedge-rows. It occurs to me that the same compliment can be paid to our purgatives. W. S. Gilbert in the ludicrous effusions of the aesthetical Bunthorne made good use of the medical chest. He pictured

45

> The writhing maid, lithe-limbed,
> Quivering on amaranthine asphodel

and the poet's dilemma

> How can he paint her woes
> Knowing as well as he knows
> That all can be set right with calomel?

He is conscious also of the charms and therapeutic value of 'the amorous colocynth' among others,

> Knowing as well as he knows
> That they are only uncompounded pills.

We may add another, senna.

The essence of calomel is chemical (mercurous chloride) not floral. But to the ear it sounds a floral note. Cascara comes from the bark of a Spanish tree. Colocynth, supplying a remedy known to the ancient Greeks when costive, is the bitter apple. Othello mentions it with its Spanish name of coloquintada. Macbeth is given knowledge of senna, an Arabian shrub whose pods contain potency. He talks of it in a way that suggests a prescience of chemical warfare,

> What rhubarb, senna, or what purgative drug
> Will scour these English hence?

Have we an internal hint in these references that Shakespeare was being dosed while he wrote these plays of adjacent years? His mind had never been sluggish and was not so at the time. But brain and bowels are not always in rhythm.

It is not so easy to make music of rhubarb, whose origin was in China and Tibet. It drifted west to fill our market-gardens with what some regard as a revolting mixture of string and acid. On its way it picked up the mediæval Latin title of Rhabarbarum. Evidently it was thought a barbarous plant, a view

46

with which I sympathise. My opinion of rhubarb was not improved on learning during some rhubarb research that it was the basis of one of my childhood's loathings, Dr Gregory's Powder. The odious stalk can be rescued by canning, which sweetens it. Sieved, it can be made into an agreeable Rhubarb Fool. But it is not for the versifiers.

There is also ipecacuhana whose alien title denotes 'a low or creeping plant causing to vomit'. It is not an obvious ingredient in a song but Gilbert, rhyming it with Havannah, wrote

> When people dine no kind of wine beats
> ipecacuhana,
> But common sense suggests
> You keep it for your guests.

It is inhuman counsel since this formidable shrub's qualities are not only emetic but purgative and diaphoretic. The last adjective means 'causing to sweat'. The song occurs in Gilbert's operetta *His Excellency* produced by Mr George Edwardes at the Lyric Theatre in 1894 and little known now because Sullivan did not contribute the music. The first line runs 'Oh what a fund of jocund fun lies in harmless hoaxes'. Harmless? Fortunately the Victorian vogue of practical jokes, spoof as it was sometimes called, has passed.

Returning to colocynth, I do not know that I have ever consumed it. Perhaps it has been ignorantly swallowed in some compounded dose. In any case it comes pleasantly to my ear amid the soothing lilt of

> Senna, cascara, colocynth, calomel.

As Kipling said of the flowers

> Almost singing themselves they run.

47

Conversatzione

In my boyhood and early youth I sometimes escaped church-going to attend Sunday gatherings in a building called a Conservatoire. The name was forbidding. I was not a Tory and I did not go there to be converted by Conservative speakers. The meeting-hall which carried this formidable name was in fact rented to people of all opinions including an Ethical Society whose visiting orators were radical in politics and sceptical about religion. Its members, as the Society's title indicated, sought the altitudes of good behaviour. Poems which counselled the pursuit of freedom and virtue combined were sung as secular hymns. These I did not relish but the speakers were congenial, none more so than Granville Barker who told us about Bernard Shaw with gusto, charm, and an admirable delivery of some Shavian excerpts. Nothing conservative about that.

The dictionary defines a Conservatoire as 'a public establishment for special instruction in music and declamation'. I suppose that during the week there was much teaching of the piano and earnest singing lessons for those who had operatic ambitions surging within them. There would also be introductions to rhetoric for those seeking to be platform orators. It was a highly cultural as well as, on Sundays, an ethical venue, as its owners might have liked it to be called. It could also be hired by hosts and hostesses wishing to hold a Conversatzione. That Italianate title was in tune with the lofty purposes of the establishment since it describes 'a soirée or other assembly of an intellectual character in connection with literature, art, or science'. I remember being taken to a party so named in a private house where there was more refreshment of the questing mind than catering for physical appetites.

The Conversatzione was a form of entertainment favoured by Trollope's Mrs Proudie. 'When we are hungry', said a clergyman's wife, 'we do all have sensual propensities.' This observation was by no means congenial to Mrs Proudie who thought that 'a conversatzione would give no play to sensual propensity nor occasion that intolerable expense which the gratification of sensual propensities too often produces. She felt that the word was not all that she could have desired. It was a little faded by old use and present oblivion and seemed to address itself to that portion of the London world that is considered blue rather than fashionable. But nevertheless there was a spirituality about it which suited her and one may also say an economy'.

There was in fact no gastric gratification for Mrs Proudie's conversationalists who strangely included Lord Dumbello who was incapable of utterance on any topic except the material and not much on that. The guests were to 'group themselves' and speak of higher things while tea and cake were sparingly passed round. Lord Dumbello did not stay long.

It is interesting to notice Trollope's use of blue for dull or solemn. That adjective has been replaced by square. Blue has had a curious history. Blue skies are cheerful in popular song but a fit of 'the blues' is now the depth of gloom. Blue jokes are dirty ones and not at all suited to the parley of a Conversatzione or the atmosphere of a Conservatoire.

The nearest thing to a Conversatzione in Dickens is in the entertainment offered by Mrs Bayham Badger in *Bleak House*. That much-married devotee of science described the lavishly communicated erudition of her previous husband, Professor Dingo. 'The class attendant of Professor Dingo's lectures

49

D

was a large one, and it became my pride, as the wife of an eminent scientific man seeking herself in science the utmost consolation it could impart, to throw our house open to the students, as a kind of Scientific Exchange. Every Tuesday evening there was lemonade and a mixed biscuit, for all who chose to partake of those refreshments. And there was science to an unlimited extent.'

('Remarkable assemblies those, Miss Summerson,' said Mr Badger reverentially. 'There must have been great intellectual friction going on there, under the auspices of such a man!')

It is not to be supposed that the friction of minds produced many illuminating sparks when Mrs Proudie was the hostess. After some terse remarks on the weather, 'We cannot always be eating', she said to Lord Dumbello who replied 'No, not always'. The clash and flash of minds got no further. Decidedly it was an occasion 'more blue than fashionable'.

Mrs Proudie thought in 1860 that the word conversatzione was 'faded by old use and present oblivion', but it did not immediately vanish. Guests were bidden to such a function half a century later and there may still be Conservatoires where soirées with conversation and mental friction continue along with tutorials in music and declamation.

Credibility

In times of political confusion we get abundance of reports which are not to be trusted. Of some such rumours I have just heard a broadcaster say that 'Credence cannot be given to them'. That solemn way of putting it reminds me that credibility, now a vogue word, is being confused with credit or standing. When a political correspondent writes sceptically of a Minister's credibility he is not intending to call the Right Honourable gentleman a liar. He may have his reasonable suspicions as to complete veracity in answers to 'Questions in the House'. But in general throwing doubts on a politician's credibility implies that he is on his way down and possibly out. It is his reputation and not his actual words that is causing scepticism.

This use of credibility has become so common that Mr William Hardcastle, the brusque and breezy introducer of the B.B.C. programme *The World at One,* paused for a moment to interject 'That word again' when the credibility of some Westminster 'high-up' was in his script. One speaker doubted the credibility of the economic blockade of Rhodesia. When he said that the blockade was a fact. Its degree of success was disputable. It was certainly credible because it was going on, unless that adjective has changed its meaning to effective.

A phrase frequently used is 'the credibility gap'. At the time of writing the Prime Minister was alleged to be sunk in that land or gulf of No Belief. He was not alone in that discreditable cavern. British politicians of all three parties, we were told, had become the shameful object of general scepticism. They were all accused of lacking credibility. This does not mean that they were incessant and incurable liars, but the current use of credibility does suggest that like bankrupts they had run out of credit and that their promises, like dud cheques, bounced. Their 'gab' is of a Britain revived and solvent. But between their television patter and the achievement lay, deep as the Grand Canyon, the gap. At this the nation might reasonably gape. To gape is to have a gap in the mouth. A gaper yawns as well as stares.

51

Swift wrote

> She stretches, gapes, unglues her eyes
> And asks if it is time to rise.

He might have been describing the bored and un-believing Britannia of 1969.

Creep

In Aldous Huxley's *Point Counter Point* first pub-lished in 1928, there are several mentions of feeble and nasty people as creeps. That name for them seems to have disappeared. They are now drips and wets. The creep of forty years ago could have been so called for two reasons. Either he was so humble and fawning that he slunk in a disgusting way into any company that he joined. Or he was a sly con-spiratorial type who made people's flesh creep with his repulsive presence. Huxley's odious, corrupting character Spandrell is a creep of that kind at least to the readers of the book. Lucy Tantamount, the gay and seductive millionairess, did not find him creepy in the shiversome way. Spandrell himself speaks of creeps, having in mind, I think, the drips rather than the deliberate and perverted scoundrels of which he is a gruesome example. The supreme creep of both kinds in English fiction is Uriah Heep who both crawls and conspires.

The phrase 'making one's flesh creep' or 'giving one the creeps' is curious because it is usually applied to sensations of terror. Plays, films and stories designed to frighten and horrify do not make one creep in the physical sense, i.e. 'to move with the body prone and close to the ground as a reptile'. My boyhood's principal horror-creep was Guy Boothby's Dr Nikola whose sinister doings made me rather sit up than writhe on the floor. Nor do I find that the entertainments now announced as spine-chillers have any effect on the vertebrae.

Influenza creates shivers and shakes more effectively than any literary or theatrical assault on the nerves. The dictionary suggests that we are said to get 'the creeps' because a tale of villainous cruelty makes us think of creeping creatures, the creepy-crawlies who approach or settle on our bodies, first unnoticed and then abominated. But I do not think that Spandrell's creeps were Satanic and serpentine. Slugs, perhaps.

D

Dicky

There was a time when that abundantly genial comedian, Stanley Lupino, could coax a vast audience at the London Hippodrome into joining in his chorus-song, 'Let's all sing like the birdies sing'. Dicky-birds stood for health and high spirits. Why in that case should we say that we are feeling a bit dicky when the day comes in with a sinking feeling and the consequent moans and groans.

Our words, not all of them slang, describing illness are strangely mixed. Chipper means fit and well.

53

Chippy means the reverse. We are simultaneously
done-up and run-down. We say that we are 'out of
sorts'. What sorts and why do we lack them? We need
not be suffering from a heavy night's drinking to feel
groggy. A knock or a blow can produce that condition.
The adjective is specially applied to horses weak in
the foreleg and wholly innocent of alcoholic excess
or race-course doping.

I do not now hear complaints of being seedy. I
remember in my boyhood that my elders used that
name for feeling poorly. When applied to certain types
it could also mean shabby and second-rate. There is
an anecdote about Frank Harris told in a club of
which I am a member. When he was being entertained
there his host suggested that the claret which he
ordered was quite a good one. This awkward guest
replied 'I suppose it's all right for the seedy type of
chaps you get here.'

For solemn excuses we have indisposed. The
recipient of an unwanted invitation pleads indisposi-
tion. The word has two meanings and signifies both
unwillingness and unfitness. The mixture of dickiness
and disinclination aptly sums up the sensations of
one who has risen wearily with no liking for the
burdens and engagements of the day ahead. It is odd
to find Shakespeare using indisposed for out-of-sorts.
King Lear contrasted 'the indisposed and sickly fit'
with 'the sound man'. Sickly fit is peculiar to our ears
but the text of the play is frequently confused which
is understandable if some of it was written, as seems
likely, during the tour which took the company to
Dover and its cliffs. A manuscript, worked on during
jog-trot journeys and fit-up performances, might be
a bit dicky.

There is a scribbled jotting of John Aubrey's whose
application is disputed. It probably indicates that
Shakespeare was no addict of long, gay nights (he had

a lot of better things to do) and we are told that when invited to a party 'writ he was in paine'. Since he used the word indisposed in a play he could have employed it also in his social evasions. 'Master Shakespeare regrets that he is indisposed.'

Dicky has had an astonishing number of meanings. It has been 'an officer in commission'. It has been not only a bird of either sex but a male donkey; it has been a detachable shirt-front, a child's bib, and a leather apron. It has been a seat at the back of a coach or a motor-car. Eric Partridge quotes from *The Athenæum* of 1870 'We cannot even guess why a Liverpool man is called "a Dickey Sam". Now the Merseyside Sam is a scouse. Thackeray wrote of 'things going all dicky'. There are 'clever dicks' and detective dicks and for folk-speech specialists there is the mystery of 'Master Dick's hat-band'. That symbol of oddity Eric Partridge describes as 'an intensive tag of chameleonic sense and problematic origin'. The dickies are indeed chameleons, saurian reptiles who changed the colour of their skin and, according to Hamlet, could, like Parliamentary electors, feed on air 'promise-crammed'. For Hamlet 'things had gone all dicky'.

Dollar

In March 1968 the vicissitudes of pounds and dollars were head-line news. The Almighty Dollar, a phrase used by Washington Irving but not necessarily invented by him, was losing its long unchallenged power. The 'Billion Dollar Country' was over-spending its billions. It is odd that Shakespeare should have mentioned dollars before the Pilgrim Fathers sailed.

He twice introduced into his text a pun on dollar and dolour (grief). The first quip is in *Measure for Measure* where Lucio and a First Gentleman are jesting obscenely about the financial and physical afflictions incurred in Mistress Overdone's brothel. Since the scene is Vienna thalers could be expected.

The second occasion is the Conspiracy Scene in *The Tempest* where the Italians shipwrecked in the West Indies again link dollars and dolours but with no bawdy significance. Ducats would have been plausible in their vocabulary, but Shakespeare liked, more than we do, this kind of play on words. The third reference to dollars occurs most curiously in *Macbeth*. His was eagle-country, it is true, but unlikely to have complicated currency problems. What was the exchange value of a dollar in the time of King Duncan of Scotland and his murderous successor? Certainly he was collecting what is called 'a packet'. The speech of 'the bleeding Sergeant' in the second scene of the first act is usually delivered at such a pace in a theatre that the dollars mentioned are not noticed.

Wars were then commercial as well as military exercises: the combatants were realistic in calculation of rewards, however romantic the poetic reporting of their prowess. The prize captured was what Macbeth might have called in a later Scottish idiom one of the 'high heid yins', a monarch or a general who could be ransomed for a handsome price. Says Ross to Duncan after the Scottish victory

> Sweno, the Norway's king, craves composition,
> Nor would we deign him burial of his men
> Till he disbursed, at St Colmes-inch,
> Ten thousand dollars to our general use.

The Nordic corpses might rot unless the dollars were produced. So a kind of blackmail could be added

56

to the crimes of Macbeth before he became a murderous criminal. He could, however, plead that this demand for cash down was according to normal custom and the ancient etiquette of war.

That the mediæval dollar was the English name for the German thaler is common knowledge. Less familiar is the fact that it was also the English name for the peso or Spanish 'piece of eight' largely used in the British North American colonies at the time of their revolt. The first settlers in New Amsterdam would speak with memories of a Dutch or German thaler while others applied the term to a Spanish relic. To the English it became a nick-name for the five shilling piece. E. C. Bentley introducing Damon Runyon to the English reader refused to include a glossary because he regarded such an addition to American novels and stories as almost offensive, implying that 'the kind of slang in question was an unintelligible lingo of barbarians'. But in Runyon's case he did think it useful to interpret the dollar slang and explain that 'a thousand dollars are a grand, or a G; a hundred dollars, a yard, or a C; ten dollars, a sawbuck; five dollars, a finnif, a fin, or a pound note; two dollars, a deuce; one dollar, a buck, or a bob'. So Sweno's ransom yielded ten G's and a thousand sawbucks.

E

Ecumenicity

There has been, I read in *The Times,* a notable example of ecumenicity. With a praiseworthy display of Christian fraternity and sorority Roman Catholics, members of the Church of England, and Nonconformists have worshipped at Westminster under the same roof. The O.E.D. accepts the erudite reporter's noun, but rejects his spelling. According to its orthography Ecumenical should be Oecumenical.

If that is so, why should there not be a science of Political Oeconomy? Both words start with the Greek for home. This gave rise to the idea of all human settlements united in a single Oeconomy which became the name for the whole inhabited world. There is further confusion. While the divines have kept the 'u' and have Ecumenical occasions the theorists of trade and finance have decided on 'o' and are Economists. But there appears to be no word Economicity to describe the latter party's academic subject or, at a lower level, the practice of the shopper seeking a bargain. The laymen have also avoided ecumenicity. The delegates of the United Nations do not conduct their bickering in an Ecumenical Assembly. They might show more tolerance if they did since the word should remind them (and unfortunately will not if they have no Greek) that they represent millions of ordinary folk with homes and in great need of peace and food for their families and neighbours in this jarring world. On, then, with sacred and secular Oecumenicity and may peace reign in the London School of Oeconomics.

Ember

I see in my diary that to-day, March 8th, is Ember Day. This suggests some warming activity with a poker and a coal fire since the third month is coming in icily with the kind of air once well described by the old and neglected adjective frore. But living in London I have no embers to stir. A coal-fire is illegal as well as expensive and rightly banned. The town is far cleaner and healthier without the creation of soot and smoke which, mingling with the natural mists of winter, provided us with 'the London particular'. That horror used to choke all and afflict, even lethally, those who already had bronchial trouble. The fire which gave us a cordial glow and sank to the embers of the grate was a killer as well as a comforter. There have been no dense fogs this winter.

The young who hardly remember that pestilent filth should turn to the first chapter of *Bleak House*. The Dickensian picture of Early Victorian London be-fogged makes one gasp and splutter as one reads. Amid the many nuisances of Twentieth-Century Progress, the noise, the crowds, the rush-hour travel and the traffic chaos here is one boon. But it can be retorted that petrol fumes, while they do not inspissate the air with the old fuliginous filth are no benefit to the lungs. (Did Dr Johnson ever use fuliginous for sooty? He unwittingly established inspissated as a cliché adjective for gloom.)

'The glowing embers through the room' were agreeable to Milton's Penseroso. The word has a fascinating sound. It invites to dreamy reflections in a chair by the fire. But Ember Days, as I should have known before I turned to the dictionary, have nothing to do with coals and comfort. Far from it. This Ember comes from 'the Old English ymbrine, ymb round and ryne running'. So it means a recurrent period and has been specially applied to the seasons of prayer and fasting. There are four phases of the ancient Ember discipline instituted by the Council of Placentia in A.D. 1095. The three days of supplication and abstention occur four times a year. In the spring they are the Wednesday, Thursday, and Friday after the first Sunday in Lent. But my diary disagrees with the lexicographer and orders me to pray and fast on Wednesday, Friday and Saturday. So I can take a day off on Thursday, rise from my knees and sit adequately fed and relaxed by my emberless fire, gas or electric.

F

Flannel

Flannel has been replacing waffle as a contemptuous description of a politician's evasive talk. I read that the self-justifying speech of a Minister in a fix was 'nothing but flannel'. The word is Welsh, a corruption of gwlanen, the adjectival form of gwlan, wool. Welsh oratory is usually forcible. Lloyd George in the fiery radicalism of his early career was no wrapper-up of his opinions about the wicked rich, especially those of ducal rank. His famous or notorious Limehouse speech put that part of East London beside Billingsgate in the vocabulary of abusive terms. No verbal gwlan for him.

Falstaff in the last scene of *The Merry Wives of Windsor* called Sir Hugh Evans 'the Welsh flannel', meaning presumably the Welsh fool. The latter could not possibly have been accused of waffling or talking flannel in his remarks about the now completely humiliated knight whom he described as 'Given to fornication and to taverns and sack and wine and metheglins and to drinkings and swearings and starings, pribbles and prabbles'. There was nothing woolly in that. Metheglin was a kind of spiced and medicated mead, a liquor much favoured by the Tudor Welsh. Prabbling was the Evans version of brabbling which meant cavilling, making paltry quarrels, and bringing fractious actions at law. Staring, one may assume at women, seems a minor form of indulgence among the others listed. Falstaff's answer was dignified.

'Well, I am your theme. You have the start of me. I am dejected. I am not able to answer the Welsh flannel.'

In the choice of clothes flannel has been much ousted. 'Always wear flannel next your skin' was a command based on the absorbency of perspiration. A cotton vest was regarded as dangerous and certain to cause chills. My boyhood was a procession of gwlan from the bedroom pyjamas to the undervest and the grey flannel suit. And so on to the flannel 'bags' of youth.

It has been realised that lighter and artificial fabrics are not fatal to health. Yet, when I take a walk in a shiversome easterly gale I believe that my legs would be better protected in the old way. When rough winds from Russia shake the bails off the wickets of the May-time cricketer, who may have just arrived from a tropical climate, I trust that he has flannel next the skin. But when the sun shines I welcome the escape into our less cumbrous and easily washable and drip-dry clothing of to-day.

I do not much like the word Nylon. It suggests a mixture of Neon lighting and the Pylons of the Electricity Boards. But the sound of Terylene comes pleasantly to the ears. The name brings rhythm to the wardrobe and could flutter gracefully in a Sonnet.

Frame

Yorkshire pleasantly preserves in common use some Elizabethan and Jacobean English. There is the verb frame, for example, meaning to show ability. In Keighley's weekly paper a columnist who signs himself 'Northerner II' reminded me that it was so used by the translators of the Authorised Version of the Bible. It occurs in the passage about the word Shibboleth in the Book of Judges (12.7). Those Ephraimites who had survived a disastrous battle with the men of Gilead at the passages of Jordan, still a river of tragedy and blood-shed, were allowed to cross in safety if they could pronounce the word Shibboleth correctly. The unfortunate Jephthah failed in the test. 'He could not frame to pronounce it right' and so his blood joined the water of that calamitous stream. 'Northerner II' added 'We say "Coom, my lad, frame!" critically say "He has nea frammation about him" and give our most fulsome praise in admitting "He frames middlin".' His fellows of the county are not all so grudging of approval. I have heard one say of a boy that he was framing champion.

The learned but rarely inspired Elizabethan poet, Samuel Daniel, in addressing his Defence of Ryme to Lord William Herbert of Wilton wrote that he had been 'first encourag'd and fram'd thereunto by your most worthy and honourable Mother'. Daniel called Wilton, where the Countess of Pembroke entertained the wits and bards, his 'best school'. That lady was a notable promoter of 'frammation' in good prose and verse. She included in her patronage those who were framing in the simple sciences of her age. Her son also used the verb in the old sense.

Of this I was reminded by John Buxton's fascinating book on 'Sir Philip Sidney and the English Renaissance'. He quoted a letter written by Herbert when he was in disgrace for seducing (or being seduced by) Mary Fitton. He is explaining to Robert Cecil that town life is all his joy. To be pastoral might be to dodge temptation, a form of agility which did not appeal to him. What he did want to dodge was dullness. In his ardent youth he had no love for his beautiful home, perhaps too cultural and ethical for a boy whom Clarendon described as 'inordinately given to women'. If he is to be rusticated for long, he says, 'I shall turn clowne, for Justice of the Peace I can by no means frame unto and one of the two a man in the country needs must be'. They would take his meaning to-day better in Keighley than in London.

G

Glout

Few to-day would understand what was meant if they were rebuked for glouting at their neighbours. I met this word in that fascinating introduction to the Authorised Version of the Bible headed 'The Translators to the Readers' praising King James for 'his constancy, notwithstanding calumniation, for the survey of the English translations'. The King was defying the conservatives who would have no new rendering. Calumny, wrote the Translators, he had to expect because 'Whosoever attempteth anything for the publick (especially if it appertaineth to religion and to the opening and clearing of the word of God) the same setteth himself to be glouted upon by every evil eye.' To glout is to survey with a sour or sullen look. The verb survived until the eighteenth century. Horace Walpole used it of frowning and menacing clouds.

The O.E.D. describes glout as a variant of gloat which was originally a verb with optical meanings, first 'to look askance', then 'to cast amorous or admiring glances'. This is curious. What was not long ago called 'giving the glad eye' is the exact opposite of glouting. Finally gloat came to mean 'To gaze with intense or passionate (usually lustful, avaricious, or malignant) satisfaction'. Nowadays, though my two-volume O.E.D. says nothing of this, one does not visualise a nasty look when gloating is mentioned. Malignant people gloat mentally over the defeat of an opponent without necessarily watching him writhe, and the greedy can gloat over the prospect of a gourmet's feast at table without actually seeing the food and wine. When the characters in *Stalky & Co* cried 'Fids, I gloat' they had in mind the humiliation of a rival House in some tricky manœuvre or of Mr King (of Balliol) in the class-room. They were not transfixing the outwitted with a baleful stare. The glouters of old did that and it is a bodeful, menacing word for their evil eye-work. It is a pity that we have lost it. Do not dramatic critics when bored or exasperated by the play on which they are to pass judgment sit glouting in their stalls? I feel that I may have done so when I practised that profession.

Gnome

Why these gnomes of Zurich? I wonder how many of those who thus describe Swiss bankers could tell us why they use the word. The name has probably adhered to these sub-Alpine financiers because their power is resented, mainly by politicians of the Left. 'Gn' words are mostly harsh and even detestable. The gnat is an odious nuisance. To gnar is to snarl or growl, now an antique but used by Tennyson. We do not want our faces to be gnarled, 'covered with protuberances, distorted and twisted'. We gnash our teeth and we, or our dogs, gnaw crusts and bones. Gneiss is one of the toughest of rocks. A gnoff was a boor or lout. The gnomes are in a grim and gritty company.

Yet the Grecian gnome, which may be pronounced

with one or two syllables, is also a maxim, proverb, or aphorism and frequently a shrewd or witty one. The gnomic authors who write or collect these pithy observations provide pleasant as well as instructive reading. The *Trivia* of Logan Pearsall Smith make slim, handy and entertaining bed-side books. Bernard Shaw's *The Revolutionist's Handbook,* which he included with the text of *Man and Superman* curtly and pungently condenses what he says elsewhere at the full stretch of his excellence in pamphleteering prose. After struggling with a long-winded book it is a relief to meet the brevity of the gnomologist, little though one may like that title for his occupation.

The Zurich gnomes, whatever their literary style, are accurately named in one way since the original gnomes of ancient mythology were 'spirits fabled to inhabit the interior of the earth and to guard its treasures'. They were not spirits only; they had bodies, but not much of them. The gnomes were as small in size as they were large in power, a pygmy breed. One does not expect the potentates of Swiss banking to be dwarfs, or as small or as beautiful as a humming-bird which is another creature to whom the name of gnome has been given in America. An additional avian gnome of the U.S.A. is the small owl. This suggests sagacity. That the treasure-guarding gnomes of Zurich are sagacious is probably true, but wisdom is not what creditors most like when they are looking for a loan. The gnomes make them gnar and gnash a tooth.

Gorblimey and Gorbelly

A proletarian oath and once a military cap unpopular with senior officers. It was worn contrary to War Office Dress Regulations. The gorblimey or slouch

effect was achieved by pulling the solid material out
of the cap so that it became loose and baggy and gave
a rakish look. It appealed in the 1914-18 war to those
for whom T. W. H. Crosland wrote a justly applaud-
ing poem.

> They're first in the ranks of the Suicide Club
> His Majesty's Second Lieutenants.

First over the top into the shambles of the Somme
they could be excused a vagary in their head-wear
while in training or on leave. For those favouring
gorblimeys a tragically brief life was a familiar
portion.

Gorblimey was not at that time a new name for
a loose and sloppy form of head-wear. In H. G.
Pelissier's pre-war Follies a comedienne sang

> My old man's a Fireman
> On an Elder Dempster boat,
> He wears a bleedin' muffler
> Around his bleedin' throat.

Or was bleedin' too close to the bloody then forbidden
on the stage. Perhaps it was blinkin'.

Above the muffler he had 'a little gorblimey hat'.
That presumably was the storm-proof article better
known as a souwester, which the Fireman wore when
he sought relief on his share of the deck after being
roasted at his stoking job. Or was it a slouch-cap
for use on shore? Slang is elastic.

Elderly staff-officers vexed with obesity (the Brass
Hats who stirred the rage of Siegfried Sassoon)
might in a previous age have been called gorbellied.
The prefix Gor was not only a mild profanity in oaths
involving the deity. It was also a material magnifier.
Gorbellied was naturally in Falstaff's vocabulary but
he did not apply it to himself. The knaves given the
adjective are the Travellers whom he helped to rob
at Gadshill. That address brings Dickens to mind.

His gorbellies could be genially paunchy like Pickwick or grossly swollen like Mr Crook in *Bleak House* who perished of internal combustion.

Groovy

Groovy has become 'trendy'. Has it the same implication of approving a trend or fashion? I discussed the point with my literary agent, Margaret Stephens of A. D. Peters. She thought that to call a person or thing groovy was to commend it, if trendy is an adjective of praise. I feel that it ought to suggest stodginess and a stick-in-the-hole character.

> There was a young man who said 'Damn'!
> At last I've found out that I am
>   A creature that moves
>   On predestinate grooves,
> In fact not a bus, but a tram.

Thus Monsignor Ronald Knox, if the attribution is correct, 'limericked' the despondent atheist, determinist, fatalist, or possibly Calvinist. To be thus grooved does not indicate one of the brighter young people recently called trendy and seen as swinging. It is true that trams, when the driver was able to accelerate, were apt to swing a bit, but they did not, with normal luck, ungroove themselves to the public peril. I suppose that the word tram must now be explained for the benefit of the young. How long ago was it that the last of them followed its clanging predestinate course?

British Railways have lately proved insufficiently groovy. The increasing tendency of trains to topple off the track is frightening. If they are passenger trains travelling at the new heightened speeds there can be a terrible disaster. If a goods' train, or part of it, wobbles over its crew are endangered. If they are happily unharmed the line is blocked and there are maddening delays for other trains still erect and full of people hoping to get somewhere sometime. The management of B.R. provides its usual apology and a groovy kind of excuse. Trains should be advertisements for the doctrine of predestination which is questionable in faith and philosophy but valuable in the ordering of public transport.

Grotty

I have just heard a B.B.C. commentator on the news speak of someone as grotty. Before that I had seen the word printed in the slang of the time. The suggestion was of annoyance and indignation.

Many words beginning with 'gr' have a sad and sour flavour. It is true that the catalogue includes grace, grand, and gratitude. But the mass of melancholic and misanthropic terms makes a growling start. We resent things grey, grim, grimy, gritty, grubby and gruesome. In vexation and frustration we grind our teeth, grizzle, groan, grouse, grumble, and grunt. If grottiness is admitted the fractious and peevish types are further and suitably represented.

Grotty might be connected with a grotto. This was a grot to T. E. Brown when he discovered in his God-wottery poem the divine presence in gardens. Thus the grotty person or cavern-fancier might be one who happily prefers solitude and is more of a pacific hermit than a hostile character. Some anchorites manage to let cheerfulness intrude. In the Stone Age the artistic grotties may have been merry enough with their lively mural paintings. But other diggers-in have tended to be misanthropes. In that class Timon of Athens was an early and notable example of the railing recluse, as grotty as any growler of them all.

The second letter does much of the grumbling work. 'R' is often what Max Beerbohm liked to call rebarbative. Substitute the liquid 'l' and there is a striking change. We gladly watch a river gliding and glowing or gleaming in the sun or glimmering with a glassy sheen under the moon. We gloat over glorious sights and achievements. The adjective glamorous has been cruelly over-worked and has been demoted from magical to merely sex-appealing. The night club has its Glamour Girls, but its patrons are far from grotty when faced with their presence. They may even merit the Carrolline adjective galumphing.

H

Hebdomadal

During my study of Oxford University's constitutional reforms proposed, accepted, and rejected, it occurred to me that, while I had often heard of its Hebdomadal Council, I was vague about the origin of its name. A Hebdomas, it seems, is the number seven or a group of seven. A Hebdomad is the space of seven days. So a Hebdomadal Council, which might have seven members, should and usually does meet weekly. The O.E.D. includes the further information that in some Gnostic systems a Hebdomad is 'a group of seven super-human beings, also a title of the Demiurge' (Supreme Being or Maker of the World). Hebdomadal Councillors could hardly ask for more. But the Oxonian exaltation has been contradicted in the practice and parley of Westminster. 'Hebdomadal politicians' were described by Burke as those 'who run away from their opinions without giving us a month's notice'. A month? Burke apparently did not know the meaning of a Hebdomas. His allusion to rapid reversal of ideas and policies was most pertinent a fortnight before this was written when the Prime Minister and his Chancellor of the Exchequer, having vowed never to devalue the pound, had to eat their words with a speed and elasticity of mind which exposed economists to the charge of being hebdomadal. Should any tradesmen of Oxford city be faithful to the lingo of their university they might inform their patrons that 'Accounts are rendered hebdomadally'.

Homuncule

Max Beerbohm, with Charterhouse and Oxford behind him, was no autodidact, but he had an early habit of injecting into English the vocabulary of the classics. His Latinisms were many. In a previous book, *A Ring of Words,* I mentioned Gongorism, 'an affected and pedantic style characterised by the abuse of Latinisms, accumulations of metaphors and extravagant neologisms'. In his earliest work Max Gongorised happily. He described jockeys, for example, as 'homuncules scudding o'er the vert'. To call the turf the vert is preciosity but homuncules is an accurate description of midgets. Apart from the little men of big renown and large rewards on the racecourse, there were or are supposed to have been homuncules artificially created by the old alchemists and then bottled for preservation.

I was reminded of Max and his vocabulary, in which fascinated eyes are said to be 'ensorceled', by reading Somerset Maugham's early novel *The Magician* first published in 1908 and re-issued in a Penguin edition in 1967. In the new preface, called 'A Fragment of Autobiography', Maugham explained that this story was written after he had met in Paris Aleister Crowley who was 'dabbling in Satanism' and thus suggested the figure of Oliver Haddo in this curious book which reminds one of the Gothic romances and Horror Stories fashionable at the end of the eighteenth century. Of his early style Maugham disapproved, calling it 'lush and turgid'. Maugham admitted having had a Gongorist phase before he achieved the conspicuously clear, simple, and un-adorned prose of his later fiction.

Homuncules or homunculi mentioned in *The Magician* were said to have been first manufactured in the Tyrol in 1775 by an aristocrat with a taste for 'ensorcelment', Count von Kuffstein, with the aid of an Italian mystic and rosicrucian, the Abbé Gelon. The creatures were kept in strong bottles. No more than a span, (nine inches) in length at first, they throve when the bottles were buried under cart-loads of manure and sprinkled with a magic liquor. Fed on human blood they grew larger and also grew beards. Their faces were horrible and fiendish.

Maugham's Haddo continued the nauseous experi-

72

ment. Exposure to the air was fatal and accidents, which we may regard as fortunate, ended the Tyrolese experiment. Haddo, a corpulent giant with a passion for the breeding of homuncules, came to a suitably violent end and was finally incinerated in his own fantastic work-shop. It was an extraordinary story to have come from Maugham's exact and realistic mind.

Imaginings of tiny creatures, whether natural pigmies or produced by sundry forms of black magic, have been popular. Tom Thumbs recur in folk-fancy. The curiosity about abnormalities made dwarfs valuable assets for the showmen of the old fair-grounds where the taste for spectacle was crude and deformities were exhibited as great attractions. In my boyhood I could see for a penny or two a natural homuncule, a minikin man sharing a booth with the enormous and bearded Fat Lady at Bank Holidays on Hampstead Heath. Now all the fun is in mechanised motion which makes it monotonous, noisy, and boring but less obnoxious to sensibility.

One does not expect to meet a team of scampering midgets in the Music Halls as I did in my youth when they were considered a great attraction. But not long ago I was told by an old vaudeville dancer that she had received a letter from her daughter who had followed in her mother's nimble steps. It said 'We are a great happy party at the Hippo this week. I am up to my arse in dwarfs'. If she had been a Beerbohm reader she could have called them homuncules scudding o'er the boards. There is one of the species in J. B. Priestley's lively and much liked novel of the old Palaces of Varieties, *Lost Empires*. He assists an Illusionist and, by this link with stage-sorcery and magic, fits into that side of the homuncular picture.

73

Hum-Drum

When I asked a friend how his life was going he
answered 'Hum-drum'. There was no doubt about
his meaning. He was having a dull time. On consult-
ing authority I found that there could be a noun as
well as an adjective. A hum-drum was old slang for
a husband or wife, but my friend probably did not
know that (few do) and was certainly not alluding to
married life. He is an actor and a good one; but his
profession, whatever its lucky or well-merited strikes,
has its disappointing patches. There are hum-drum
intervals while new plays, films, or television series
are being planned and cast.

His choice of a description for uneventful days set
me wondering about the origin of this curious word.
Neither of its components brings a dreary vacuum
to mind. We talk of a town humming with activity.
Things excitedly on the move are said to be 'fairly
humming'. The drum is a martial instrument; it may
be muffled for mourning, but generally it calls for
energetic action. There is a furious and sanguinary
battle in *The Drums of the Fore and Aft* Kipling's
vivid and poignant story of two juvenile scamps who
become the heroes of a lethal day.

It is true that nervous or baffled speakers are said
to hum and haw, but the other meanings of hum
or drum suggest a bustling life or a military summons.
None the less, as a husband, I am doubtless a hum-
drum.

Hypergamy

A critic discussing the long neglected and recently
revived plays of D. H. Lawrence wrote of the

hypergamous relations of the characters. I take it that he was alluding to marriages interrupted by the amatory deviations of the over-sexed and under-satisfied. (The old libertarians used to talk of Free Love but that is too simple for our permissive age with its large assortment of the permissibles.) But hypergamy does not mean excess of marriage or of mating. It is defined by O.E.D. as 'marriage with one of equal or superior caste; in reference to Hindu custom'. This statement is puzzling and seems to contradict itself. Equals and superiors are opposites. To be hyper is to be super. The young women who describe all things warmly enjoyed and approved as super do not, in my experience, call them hyper since few of them have studied Greek, but it may be that some reading the classics at the universities do exclaim 'Positively hyper, my dear'.

Returning to the Laurentian characters I should fairly call Lady Chatterley's game-keeper an addict of hyperadultery. If we are to accept one part of the dictionary's definition 'marriage with one of superior caste' the high time for the hypergamous girl was Edwardian London when the young aristocrats went for their wooing to the stage doors of the old Gaiety and Daly's theatres. The feminine stars or members of the chorus, who had to be photogenic since it was the age of the Picture Post-Card, then achieved hypergamy with some frequency. Since the nobility has been taxed out of its opulence the acquisitive beauty, now a dish, can do better financially with the pace-setting member of a Top-of-the-Pops group. A titled husband, with less hair on the head and face and less cash in the bank, may provide what may now be called 'Social escalation'. But to be in Debrett is not necessarily to be 'in the money'. Hypergamy must move with the times.

I

Idioticon

This suggests a lexicon of lunatic jabber or a dictionary of words drawn from documents in madness. It is in fact a guide to dialect 'containing words and phrases particular to one part of a country', a fascinating prospect for word-collectors. It is a sad thought that the word idiot which meant to the ancient Greeks a man with his own ideas, an individualist with his own private world of thought and conduct, should have been degraded to mean the idiot as we know him. We have been kinder and more sensible in our treatment of idiosyncrasy; in this case a peculiarity of mind or temperament does not indicate that its idiosyncratical owner should be sent to a mental hospital.

Poets have been thought idiots, Christopher Smart, Blake, Clare and others of less inspiration. Wordsworth's long and jingling rhyme *The Idiot Boy* is prefaced by the remark that the last stanza 'The Cocks did crow, to-whoo, to-whoo and the sun did shine so cold' was the foundation of the whole. That the sun shines cold we know on any bright east-windy day of March. This poem has two good lines

> To lay his hands upon a star
> And in his pocket bring it home.

That is what the supposedly idiot poets have often done. It is at least comforting to know that the

Idioticon has not suffered the slurs put on the name of the first Idiot, the alone-standing man who was to be the Ibsenite hero.

Image

The absurd misuse of the word image continues. Here is a sentence from an article by a woman journalist on the heating of beds in winter. The writer is maintaining that the old, kettle-filled hot-water bottle is more serviceable than the plugged-in electric blanket. She ends by saying 'The image of the hot-water bottle is being up-graded'.

So the familiar comforter of the couch, once made of stone and later of rubber, takes its place with a Prime Minister and a political party as an image-owner. Are we to look for a vast and rugged sculpture of the article which will be on display at Millbank or in one of the Parks and then up-graded by the critics as immensely significant and powerfully meaningful, and, of course, dynamic?

Imburse

I am always happy to see on a statement about any of my modestly gainful occupations the post-script 'Expenses Reimbursed'. Here is an imposing term for a refunding lawfully as well as hopefully claimed. It strikes me as odd that I am never said to be imbursed. That verb and its noun imbursement have faded away. Yet reimbursement continues in its mediæval solemnity. So does emolument.

The latter is taken to be more respectable than the brief fee or payment. It suggests an exalted occupation with a salary forwarded monthly or quarterly and yet not to be given that less august title. No manual worker paid weekly or by the job in cash would talk of his emolument. Nor, if he got something for expenses, would he think of calling it his reimbursement. There is a lofty sense of rank (call it silly snobbery if you like) in the terminology of wages and rewards. Loftiest of names for money earned is honorarium. But this is as deceitful as it is dignified since it suggests that the recipient has been working for nothing in what is called 'an honorary capacity'. An honorary secretary who gets a fee, which is often abundantly earned, should not be ashamed to admit it. If he thinks mention of a fee or salary degrading he can call it his emolument or imbursement. Yet there is no reason for giving high social status to the former. By origin an emolument means something out of the mill. It has been extracted and won by a grind and it may need more grinding to collect it when the employer is one of the Gradgrind family by nature or on the rocks by misfortune.

The Greek and Latin burse became the purse. Sir Thomas Gresham's Royal Exchange in the City of London was known for a while as the Burse. The French have retained the form Bourse. In Britain purse has prevailed except in the case of the College or Institution Bursar who may reimburse those with legitimate claims for repayment of money spent but would not imburse an undergraduate with his student's allowance. In Scotland however a scholarship is a bursary.

One of the oddities is the different usages on land and sea. The bursar on the passenger ship is a purser. Sailors are not expected to be classical scholars. There has never been any impursing or reimpursement. To be reimbursed with money owed adds to one's social status, about which I care little if the cash is there.

Another strange fact is that mention of money either produces the pomposity of the emolumentary kind or a wide variety of curious slang. The receiver of an honorarium could speak of getting his rhino, his dibs, or his lolly, but I do not think it likely. Such talk would make him purse his lips, a usage which came from tightening the purse-strings.

Incumbent

It is both surprising and unfortunate that a parish clergyman should be called its incumbent. Incumbency is defined as 'the condition of lying or pressing on something'. I am therefore the prone incumbent of my bed at night or of a couch on a lazy day. There have been incumbent or recumbent clerics in the long and often corrupt past of the Church of England, but it would be a gross libel to suggest that the clergy to-day regard their parishes as sofas and are taking life lying down. They have their challenge in the decline of faith and many are on their toes to meet it. Some do so by shedding old and baffling dogma and terminology. There is a young dislike of the old theological language. The vicar of a parish in a northern industrial town wrote to *The Times* quoting a letter from one of his flock who said that the Christian ethics were all right for him but that he could not put up with 'The Holy Ghost and all that caper'. The incumbent of that parish can hardly be regarded as a cushioned idler if he has to fight the good fight in those surroundings.

The ecclesiastical vocabulary is puzzling and must

be irritating to young people who are strange to it. What is the difference, asks the layman, between a vicar and a rector? A rector, I discover, is one 'whose tithes are not impropriate'. Impropriate as a verb means to 'annex an ecclesiastical benefice and to place tithes in other hands'. So a rector has not been expropriated. A vicar, apparently, has, and must rely on his stipend. And why should the clergy have words like benefice and stipend for a salary? Has stipend an air of sanctity? It should not since the original *stipendium* was the pay of a Roman soldier.

Then there is the mysterious Prebendary, holder of a prebendal stall in a cathedral. Prebend is taken from the Latin *præbenda* meaning 'things to be supplied'. That indicates more material gain than spiritual activity which is probably unfair. I do not doubt that there is great activity as well as devotion among Prebendaries. That there were prebendal abuses in the past is made plain in Trollope's *Framley Parsonage*. The Framley incumbent, the likeable but rash Mark Robarts, acquired a prebendal stall in Barset's cathedral through a shabby political manœuvre. This evoked a stinging leading article in the *Jupiter,* obviously the *Times*. Said the thundering writer 'Among those positions of dignified ease to which fortunate clergymen may be promoted are the stalls of the canons or prebendaries in our cathedrals. Some of these, as is well known, carry little or no emolument with them but some are rich in the good things of the world. Excellent family houses are attached to them.' Plainly a prebendal stall was then an incumbency in the comfortably recumbent sense. The *Jupiter* (this was in 1865) admitted that 'reform was busy, attaching some amount of work to the pay, and putting off of some superfluous wealth from such of them as were over full'. Reform has continued. The 'præbenda' have doubtless been better shared.

Yet the prebendal name, like that of the incumbent, bewilders. Then there are the Deans, Rural Deans, Deacons and Archdeacons. The vocabulary of the Church can be said to have historic dignity but in a sceptical, equalitarian world it does not improve what will now be called its image. Image? A hard word for Low Churchmen. The previously mentioned critic of the Paraclete, another name for his resented Holy Ghost, might again stumble in 'All that caper'.

Ironing Out

Iron has been a regular contributor to the cliché list. The Psalmist's rods of iron were once frequent in the language of retributive vengeance. The busy person always has many irons in the fire, yet he is rarely a black-smith or a washer-woman heating up for action. Most conspicuous to-day is the ironing out of problems and complications. The Chairman of a large industrial company has just spoken to his share-holders as though he were a mixture of laundryman and dentist. He was glad to tell them that 'We have ironed out our teething troubles'. That reaches the summit of Board Room absurdities. Do you wish to have infantile jaws so hotly and metallically handled? Cruelty to children and the English language are here wonderfully combined. The Chairmen's speeches, or those who write them for delivery at the Annual General Meeting, are much addicted to 'dashing away with the smoothing iron'. That metaphor comes tumbling out among the 'long, cool looks' which the directors are taking in order to cope with the teething troubles by going back to the grass

81

F

roots. I await the orator who assures his hearers that his sagacious Board is 'ironing out the winds of change'.

Ising and Izing

While waiting for television's commercial advertising to stop adding to my entertainment I learned that a brand of chocolates was all the more tasty, nourishing, and certain to increase personal energy because the solid constituents had been moisturised with pure cream. The writer of the script had decided that moistened was a participle too much of the past and that the present fashion needs longer words to commend the supposedly better article. To be snappy is sometimes the aim, but often the policy is never to use two syllables if three can be provided. So sweets would be sweeter if moisturised and not merely moistened with the lashings of cream which come streaming visibly onto the screen.

The lengthening process is elsewhere seen in the notes of political correspondents discussing Pressure Groups in Parliament. Once the Prime Minister and his Ministers were simply pressed to do this or that. Then the noun pressure was turned into a verb. So they were pressured. Now they are even pressurised. It is possible to go a step further. The dissidents and deviators from the official line are liable to undergo pressurisation to conform. They will, it is said, be disciplined and may soon, if the vogue continues, be disciplinised.

The difference between -ising and -izing is determined by the classical origin of the word in question. Those with a Latin source should have 's' and the Grecians 'z'. Accordingly we are correctly (and hopefully) said to be more civilised because our lives are better organized. But the rules are not always observed. I have seen pressurized. As the moisturised chocolates, with which I began, were glorified in words only (the pictures had no verbal captions) I could not tell whether that spelling would have been kept. I fancied that the advertiser might have believed that moisturizing or moisturization would have added to the pressurization of his sales-drive. I have also read of milk which has been (healthily) homogenized. Homogenizing should mean assimilating, but to what the milk is being assimilated remains unknown to me. However the treatment sounds suitably impressive.

Hearing of the creamily moisturised chocolates reminded me that one of the worst lines ever written by a poet whose quality was unquestionable when he kept to his natural and native speech was written by Robert Burns when he wrote of his tears that 'Something like moisture conglobes in my eye'. In this mood of composition he might have referred to his lacrimation. At least he did not tell us that his cheeks were moisturised. If the copy-writer had turned from chocolate to custard and wished to claim that so-and-so's golden compost would never go lumpy he might have imposingly announced that there was no risk of conglobisation.

K

Kex

For players of Scrabble kex is a precious word especially if double points can be scored on the two consonants. It is an antique name for the dried hemlock. John Moore mentions it in *These English Words* as one of the Elizabethan and Shakespearian survivals in the village English of his Cotswolds. It is most often heard in the plural; the children gather kecksies. They do so at their peril. With kex Socrates was poisoned and those who make the dried stem into a whistle are having dangerous fun.

In a wide-ranging and fascinating article on Shakespeare's vocabulary of flowers published in the Journal of the Royal Horticultural Society in 1964 Margaret Strickland suggested a derivation from the Welsh Cecys. So one would look for kecksies in the counties bordering on Wales; the Cotswolds and Warwickshire both had their influx of Welsh people and words. But its use has been widely dispersed. Miss Strickland has found 'dry as a kex' in Thomas Hardy and quotes two passages from the East Anglican John Clare. In his poem on Rural Fishing Clare described the children who were preferring a secular and riverside Sunday to attendance at church or chapel,

> Half-hid in meadow-sweet and keck's high flowers
> In lonely sport they pass the summer hours.

It is not a musical word though the stalk is supposed to have been used for the pipes of Pan. But it is apt for picturing the weedy wilderness of a neglected country-side such as that described by the Duke of Burgundy in *King Henry V*, the war-torn France where.

> nothing teems
> But hateful docks, rough thistles, kecksies, burs.

If a Scrabble player profitably producing kex is challenged he has ample authority for its use.

L

Lamentable

Lamentable has had a curious history. The passing of good people is lamentable as their lives have been admirable. At an early stage of the language the termination 'able' implied activity. A barking dog was called a barkable dog and in some cases that usage has remained. A capable person is one who can take a job on and not one who is easily taken in or captured. An Elizabethan poet could speak of his lamentable verses without decrying them. He would have been describing a lamenting elegy or threnody. *Adonais* is thus a lamentable masterpiece. But the word had lost that meaning by Shelley's time. It was on its way to becoming the adjective of the critic, amateur or professional, who had been bored or disgusted by a play, a book, or a film. It is not so rudely dismissive as contemptible since there is the implication of a word spoken more in sorrow than anger. The author or performer could have done better: the lament is for hope disappointed. That there should have been such expectation is something of a compliment.

Lament to me suggests a gentle suffering with no hysterical up-roar of woe. The longer lamentation does suggest a wild outcry. Shakespeare would have agreed with that. In *Macbeth* he linked 'lamentings heard i' the air' with 'strange screams of death', prophecies of dire combustion, confused events, chimneys blown down, a fevered shaking of the earth, and night-long hooting of owls. But, on the whole, mention of a lamentable poem comes smoothly to the ear. Its pains of deprivation are musical.

Our language has been well furnished with words for personal loss. Grief, sorrow, mourning, lament and suffer have the right sound for the sadness of which they tell. They add dignity to dolour. The letter 'r' brings into the background a roll of funeral drums. The Scottish coronach was the contribution of the pipers and there again the letter 'r' is poignant. Sir Walter Scott's poem called 'Coronach', not one of his best, has the advantage of repeated 'r's' in the corries and forests where the lamented hero of the Highlands made his forays.

Browning's 'wind-grieved Apennines' offer a most appropriate and effective adjective for peaks from which the pierce of icy gusts suddenly descends. I have been in Scottish corries where the epithet grievously struck the mind as the wind, coming suddenly down off some lingering patch of snow, tore at one's face. In its moan there seemed to be a coronach for some old deer-stalker or his gillie remembered in the grieving of the hills.

A change from the shiversome rocks to a cosy niche indoors is provided by the Scottish corrieneuchin. Corrie, as a corner, can be at the fireside as well as in the granite. When I met corrieneuchin I naturally consulted Jamieson and learned that 'Two old wives, talking very familiarly by themselves, are said to be corrieneuchin.' Gossip and scandal, one expects, are buzzing in the ingle-nook. There is also a noun. 'A corrieneuchin can be held in a neuk or corner.' But why limit this form of secluded chatter to the elderly and female talkers? Even young men may be seen enjoying over their beer what is sometimes called a chinwag, a word which I find lamentable in the new sense. Corrieneuchin should have Scottish whisky for its stimulant if the talk dwindles.

M

Mandarin

My morning paper is decorated with the photograph of a royal Duchess wearing what is called 'a mandarin hat'. It is 'a square job' unworthy of the handsome face below it and would, I thought, have been better suited to one of the intellectual ladies recently dubbed 'squares' by the curveting young. It seemed to be the right 'tile' for the President of a feminine Academe. The mandarin or mandarine is also 'a small sweet and richly coloured orange'. Furthermore it is a sour or acerbic (if your Cross Word has just given you that one) name for a person having authority and ponderously using it. So ancient China is widely represented.

A correspondent reminds me that Mandarin was one of the pejorative terms employed by his father, a retired naval officer with a copious equipment of dismissive slang. (How, by the way, should one pronounce the formidable word pejorative? I should put the stress on the first syllable, but I have just been listening to a B.B.C. speaker who spoke of someone using pejorrative words.) The naval captain just mentioned called cheap claret belly-whistle and spoke of any dish he thought paltry as manavalins. Manavalins meant bits and pieces of food scrounged or purloined by sailors. Among his hates were the Civil Service Mandarins, as he called them. Compared with some of his other metaphors of contempt this was mild. But it revealed the distaste of the man at sea for the chair-borne fellow at the Admiralty who determined his movements and his promotion or lack of it.

It was an accurate application to British life since the Mandarins of old China were not the aristocrats but the bureaucrats. Their name stood for 'all grades of Chinese officials, of which there were nine, each distinguished by a particular kind of button'. This suggests Trade Union leaders to us now. Presumably there was a professional organization of Amalgamated Mandarins who did themselves well at an Annual Conference. The Mandarins gave their name to the language spoken by the officials. It may have been lucid or it may have been the baffle-gab of the Pekin Barnacles.

I first met Mandarin used derisively in English in the journalism of Arnold Bennett. He was largely self-educated, a voracious book-man who had in his youth read for enjoyment and not as a critic compelled to face much that is wearisome. Bennett, when he was a critic in his later years, hit out with gusto and his praise and blame were immensely influential because written in a clear and cogent way. Lord Beaverbrook did not want a Mandarin or one of those whom A. B. Walkley used to call in *The Times* the 'Littery Gents'.

Much earlier Bennett's articles on books in *The New Age,* contributed under the pseudonym of Jacob Tonson, were my school-day's delight. He especially scorned the Professors of English Literature. He regarded them as tedious pedants who turned their fascinating subject into a wilderness of dull words and dreary valuations. The erudite bores were Mandarins to him and he banged them about while he gave an appreciative and valuable welcome to the lively young. I did not stop to think that while he was engaged in an anti-Mandarin tirade he might be sweeping one or two vivacious academics under the carpet.

He may not have been the first to bring the Chinese into the vocabulary of criticism. The Orient had been involved before. Smollett had called Dr Johnson the Grand Cham of literature. Boswell noted 'In my first edition the word was printed Chum, as it appears in one of Wilkes's Miscellanies and I animadverted on Dr Smollett's ignorance, for which let me propitiate the *manes* of that ingenious and benevolent gentleman. Chum was certainly a mistaken reading for Cham, the title of the Sovereign of Tartary, which is well applied to Johnson the Monarch of Literature.'

The doctor's verdicts on many were far from chummy. If he was indeed a Cham, explained as an obsolete form of Khan, he was never a Mandarin in Bennett's usage of the word for a dullard. Panjandrum was a word in existence while Johnson was qualifying as a Cham. It was invented by Samuel Foote as part of a string of nonsense words designed to test the memory of the actor Macklin who boasted that he could remember anything on hearing it. Panjandrum so well suited the over-lord that it has long survived Foote and his rival.

The titles for the wielders of power have included Tycoon. That word is a western mistake. It is explained as the foreigners' version of the Japanese Shogun. Tycoons operate mainly in Big Business. I have not seen the word applied to critics of the arts. Clement Scott, of the *Daily Telegraph,* was a Tycoon and a Grand Cham in his time: his influence was large but his splutterings of abusive rage when he was confronted with Ibsen's 'social realism' look absurd when quoted to-day. Bernard Shaw, devoted Ibsenite and hammer of Sir Henry Irving in the eighteen-nineties, lacked, though he might have liked, the Tycoon's domination and nobody could have been further from the Mandarin as Bennett conceived him. To the theatrical Left Wing their red-headed rebel in the staff was an 'eminence rouge'. A. B. Walkley quoted French wittily and skirted nimbly round the Shavian and doctrinal drama. He never 'chammed' His successor, Charles Morgan, in his published letters and at some grave moments could seem Mandarinic, but his notices had a saving touch of wit and grace.

The Grand Chams were nicely described by Sir Walter Scott as 'the Big Bow-Wows'. The Scots later gave them the simple and accurate name of High Heid Yins. The modern slang for the occupants of august Chairs and power-corridors is poor stuff. Talk of the Big Noises and Big Shots does not sufficiently detonate. When we have reached His Nibs we have touched bottom in the nomenclature of the top people. Personage is a term which might be more employed. There is one syllable and a world of difference between a person and a Personage. The latter does not enter a room. He imposingly arrives and listen we must.

Mesocratize

Our levellers want to democratize all manner of diverse things ranging from the regimen of Universities to the production of Shakespeare's plays.

As a member of a company closely attached to the Crown and often commanded to perform at Court Shakespeare could hardly be contemptuous of social ranking and did in fact pronounce explicitly in its favour in the long political lecture delivered by Ulysses in *Troilus and Cressida*. But one or two of the 'must-be-with-it' directors at Stratford-upon-Avon have other ideas. To suit the taste of the time Shakespeare must be democratized and this can be achieved by making the noblemen appear as noodles. I noticed in *The Shakespeare Survey* a protest at the guying of Orsino in *Twelfth Night*. A Duke, if to be justly envisaged in our democracy, must be shown as a trifling ninny. Making the V.I.P.s ridiculous would hardly have won favour for the Lord Chamberlain's Men and might have landed them in prison. But to show that our theatrical administrators are in with the times the big-wigs must be reduced to small fry.

I note elsewhere a deviation from democratization.

Professor T. H. Pear, respected authority on diction and vocabulary, in a lecture on 'Permissiveness in Speech and Manners' has remarked that 'a present aim, supported by powerful commercial interests, is to "mesocratize" rather than democratize speech'. I take it that the commercialists having something to sell on a large scale, believe that the millions of potential buyers are more likely to be coaxed into spending if they are approached as middle-class and not as proletarians. This may be happening, but when I see and hear that excellent actress Miss Kathleen Harrison commending a detergent on the television screen she is not playing up to the bourgeois. Her chat is the 'matey' kind familiar in the most ordinary homes. This seems to me to be sensible since there is usually more spending money there than in the average middle-class maisonette.

When our pre-fix for things or people in the middle is followed by a Greek word the Greek meso is the right start. Archaeologists and doctors are mesophilists in composing their professional vocabulary. Some Stone Age men were mesozoic. Our inwards are afflicted with mesogastric pains, our feet with weakness of the mesopodium. Oddly a mesoseismic convulsion does not mean a middle-sized earthquake but describes a seismic centre of greatest intensity. Mesocratize has not yet found its way into the dictionary. But I see no reason why mesocracy should not be admitted. It is a fair description of a community which is ruled neither by an aristocracy or a proletarian régime.

A novelty noted by Professor Pear is the vocal technique of the popular disc-jockey whose accent is neither quite English or quite American. 'Mid-Atlantic' he calls it. He might describe this patter of the international entertainment world as Mesoceanic. Heavily to stress the first syllable would not be unfair.

Mother

To those watching *King Lear* capably performed in the theatre the general impact is so powerful that they rarely notice peculiarities of language. How many of the myriads who have heard Lear's turbid and terrifying outcries realise that he called a hysterical seizure a mother? It occurs in the passage where he strangely and suddenly becomes a Latinist and cries

'*Hysterica passio,* down thou climbing sorrow.'

It is generally accepted that the date of the play is 1606. In 1600 Dr John Hall, a physician of high repute, had settled in Stratford and before long was courting Shakespeare's daughter Susanna whom he married in 1607. Hall wrote his clinical notes, some of which were posthumously published in 1657, in Latin. The poet may have picked up the curious name for an emotional spasm in conversation with his future son-in-law during a Stratford vacation. Mother may have been a term locally used to describe a pother, a word also used in *King Lear*.

When Lear rebukes his 'climbing sorrow' he also exclaims 'Oh how this mother swells up toward my heart'. The word hysteria comes from the Greek hysteron, the womb. The *hysterica passio* was supposed to be a feminine weakness coming from below the belt. Lear says as much with the dismissive cry of 'Thy element's below'. Mother does suggest an emotional upheaval with a smothering loss of breath and consequent mental confusion. We have the slang or dialect word moidered or moithered for this condition. Lear's kind of mother is explained in G. B. Harrison's notes

93

on the play as 'a form of suffocation, a feeling of "the heart in the mouth", and the physical result of intense emotion'. Had the maternal *hysteron* anything to do with the usage?

It has been pointed out to me by Mr Bosley, Clerk to the Governors at the Theatre Royal, Stratford-upon-Avon, that Shakespeare also used mother as a term for sexual attraction. What else can it mean in Imogen's out-cry about Posthumus? (*Cymbeline*, Act III, Scene 4).

'Some joy of Italy,
Whose mother was her painting, hath betrayed him.'

Shakespeare hated the crafts of the feminine beauty-parlour. 'God has given you one face and you make yourselves another.' Perhaps his Queen never heard that line. She would not have thanked him for it. This use of mother for rouge as well as hysteria is very curious.

The modern names for hysteria are not so dignified. Lear, we might say as he tottered towards madness, was getting a fit of the jim-jams, the jitters, or the heebie-jeebies.

Mystery

When the Beatles of world-renown produced a film called 'The Magic and the Mystery' they received what are now called abrasive comments. (Abrasive, literally meaning rubbing or scraping off, has now become a vogue-word for sharply critical or even abusive.) Not having faced the spectacle offered or listened to the noises made I abstain from criticism. But I was amused to find the word mystery applied to any entertainment provided by this Top of the Pops Group since mystery first implied a holy silence.

The mysteries of the ancient Greeks were celebrated with awe and reverence at Eleusis by the Athenians who had lost all faith in the old Olympian establishment and were not in the least affronted by seeing and hearing Zeus and his company ridiculed at the stage festivals of comedy. The word describing the mysteries came from a verb 'amuein' meaning to keep the mouth shut. Eleusis and its rites were completely 'hush-hush'. To mention the proceedings was forbidden or even unthinkable. The lips of all participants were sealed. The Masonic lodges have had a similar kind of secretive mystery. But total silence has not been preserved and a television programme has set the initiations and oaths before our eyes and ears. They have been de-mysticised as the Eleusinian procedures never were.

Mystery has been confused with ministry or service. It has been the name of a craft or profession with no need for lip-sealing. Abhorson, the executioner in *Measure for Measure,* when the bawd Pompey was offered to him as assistant, said in disgust 'He will discredit our mystery'. The Mystery Plays of the Middle Ages were so named because they were the mummings of the workers in their guilds. Their performances were religious in a narrative and sometimes jovially anecdotal and not in a mystical way. They were as public as they could be with the whole town watching the antics of the shipwrights who built a mimic Ark. But that usage has passed. Your go-to-work neighbour does not say 'I belong to the mystery of Civil Servants' whatever the nature of his possibly baffling operations.

Shakespeare used mystery in several ways, including our modern sense of a puzzle. Hamlet complains that Rosencrantz and Guildenstern will 'pluck out the heart of my mystery'. In the plentiful detective fiction the murder mysteries abound. By them we are mystified in a manner far removed from the mysticism of the contemplative or enraptured faithful. The Trappist is a true mystic if we go back to the original silence of the Greek pilgrim to Eleusis.

The adjective mysterious, if it can escape from the atmosphere of 'A funny thing happened last night' and bumps in the dark, has authentic power and splendour. When Cowper wrote in the best known of his Olney Hymns that 'God moves in a mysterious way' the word meant more to him than puzzling. When the Beatles chose as a title 'The Magic and the Mystery' their ambition may have been laudable but their choice of words rash. However, they are not, I think, classical scholars and can hardly know that a mystery began with keeping mum.

N

Neurypnology

New sciences or new forms of humbug arrive as often as germs in January. I am invited to 'write with confidence' to a Neurypnologist for whose therapeutic treatment the fees are not stated in his promise of the soothing to come. The first part of his wisdom is plain. He will ease my nervous tensions. But what then? Has an 'h' dropped out of his second syllable? Will he hypnotise? There is no certainty as to that. What he does promise is to control my 'fears, anxieties, and bad habits'. I can therefore turn to him (and shall not) to cure me of sloth, smoking of cigarettes, delay in answering letters, and all the reluctances of the ordinary comatose fellow.

The company in which the Neurypnologist makes his appeal for custom is curious, including a Detective Service for confidential inquiries, a Friendship and Marriage Bureau (Catholics welcomed), Pregnancy Tests, and the supply of Successful Family Planning Energy Tablets. Since Family Planning is usually a name for limitation of offspring I am surprised that increase of energy by tabloid doses is thought likely to produce a reduction of our still growing population. But the placing of the Neurypnologist's advertisement seems suitable. By the time that the reader has employed a Private Eye, worried about a partner in marriage, pregnancy, and the need for Energy Tablets neurasthenia may have reached a stage at which any 'ypnology' is urgently required.

O

Orientated

When the staff of the National Trust produced a new form of Newsletter for their supporters they received what is called 'a gratifying mail-bag'. Among the congratulations was a letter which praised that excellent organisation for becoming 'more consumer-orientated'. Preservation of Britain's natural and historic beauty is the purpose of the Trust. It seems that not all its members are dedicated to care of the English language. It also seems that the pomposities of commercial sales talk have infected even those who are rightly concerned with the survival of the best in building and landscape.

This use of oriented and quite commonly orientated instead of directed or aimed at has become a tiresome nuisance. Why are we always supposed to be facing east? Are we never occidented? I have seen an English industrial product described as 'orientated to the American market'. Orientation fascinates some literary critics as much as the merchant in search of markets. The writers whom they discuss are frequently orientated and sometimes in very queer directions. When Francis Thompson wrote his Orient Ode on faith and dawn he knew what he was talking about.

The phrase quoted by the editor of the National Trust newsletter is particularly odious. As a member of the Trust I do not consider myself a customer. To subscribe to it can be called a bargain as well as a duty because it is keeping our country as decent as may be in times of barbarous alterations and destructions. If I approve of the format of the Newsletter it is not because it is oriented at my purse. I am not saying that customer is a word of which to be ashamed. It was good enough for Shakespeare and Pepys. 'No milliner can so fit his customer with gloves' is said by Autolycus in *The Winter's Tale*. (Was there here a memory of her of his father's shop in Stratford-upon-Avon? That play's Bohemia is full of Warwickshire.) But I do not think that John Shakespeare, glover, would have known what was meant if he was commended for being 'customer-oriented'.

The word customer has been badly treated. Why should he usually be spoken of as rough and tough? And the Orient, turned into a verb, has also been absurdly knocked about. No sooner had I written this than I read an advertisement suggesting that I join 'A psychoanalytically oriented group'. The group can argue in defence of their appeal that the forcing-beds of their addiction have been in Vienna and Zurich which are south-east of Britain. But the great market for psycho-therapeutic couches is surely American. It is by becoming occidented that they are most likely to receive 'a gratifying mail-bag'.

P

Pansy

It is strange that this nick-name, now somewhat out of fashion, should have been taken from the diction-ary's Viola Tricolour, otherwise called Heartsease or Love-in-Idleness, since it was considered to be a stimu-lant of bi-sexual love. Oberon, in *A Midsummer Night's Dream,* made it his spell-binding aphrodisiac in a play written for a wedding and celebrating nor-mal unions.

> The juice of it on sleeping eyelids laid
> Will make a man or woman madly dote
> Upon the next live creature that it sees.

And so it prevailed. Ophelia was accurate when she said that pansies are for thoughts. The pansy 'freak'd with jet' is an Anglicised pensée, but there are curious contradictions. The flower was named as pensive and believed to be passionate. The name Heartsease suggests a soothing influence but it was supposed to have inflammatory effects. (It was also thought to be operative on other organs than the heart since it was once recommended to sufferers from rupture.) The pansy has had its work most variously cut out.

There is uncertainy about the variant names. Love-in-Idleness suggests an infatuation of a light and transient kind and an aphrodisiac must do more than start a holiday flirtation. Pansies were also customary ingredients of love-philtres when alchemists were expected to produce a powerfully erotic dose as it did in Oberon's case.

The effects of Cupid's bolt are counter-acted in the play by the application of Dian's Bud whose title points rather to further doting than to release from adoration. Miss Strickland, on whose Shakespearian and floral wisdom I have already drawn, thinks that this was *agnus castus,* the Mediterranean's Tree of Chastity whose products were supposed to keep women cold and virtuous. What of the men? Now our dedication to sexual equality should commend fair shares in the administration of anti-erotic doses. The ancient world was little concerned with such justice but it would be a most inequitable society in which the males were sipping or being smeared with pansy-juice while the women were being treated with a conflicting medicine. In my boyhood there was a popular song about

> Pretty little pansy faces
> Growing in the garden there.

That was then no jesting allusion to epicene types

100

who, as I said, were later exposed to the pansy sneer. In our Permissive Age there might be a case for adding the Tree of Chastity to the plantations of the Forestry Commission and to the timbered lawns of our public parks.

Placebo

This Latin word for 'I shall please' had been given to a flatterer or sycophant before it was applied to a medical prescription. It is a dose ordered to keep the patient happily conscious that something is being done for him. Like a baby he needs his bottle and gets it. Placidity is thus, at least sometimes, promoted. The doctor may be aware that the contents of the bottle have little or no therapeutic value for the body. He also knows that in the cases of nervous hypochondriacs (and few of us can claim to be never fussy about our health) the placebo may not only be a harmless mixture; it may alleviate distress. It can have a psychological effect of the kind which the learned like to call euphoric.

The sufferers from placebitis are many and various. Some innocently persuade themselves that a glass of whisky will be a valuable and lasting stimulant instead of an agreeable inducement to have another and perhaps several after that. Among unmedical people there are strange beliefs. I remember being told during a prolonged attack of lumbago (slipped discs had not then been thought of) that a sovereign remedy was the string of a violin tied round my middle. I did not swallow that information but, if I had been a placebist, I might have regarded the musical equipment as powerfully medical and convinced myself of diminished pain. Another widely recommended cure for rheumatism is the wearing on the wrist of a copper band which is expected to absorb the acid in the system. People of judgment believe this and swear they have profited by their bracelet. The doctors scoff, but a physiotherapist, also sceptical, acknowledged to me that it could have a placebo value. To believe in a salve for stiffness could mitigate the trouble.

That kind of self-persuasion spreads widely. Electors are frequently imagining that a change of rulers will bring relief from affliction. The vote is a political placebo in both senses of the word. It flatters and soothes with an illusory sense of power. We feel better after a by-election when a violent swing of voting has smitten the Government. It may also be the case that a portentous medical jargon has some place-bist influence. Patent medicines are sold with included leaflets which employ a vocabulary which may be the more impressive the less intelligible it is. The polysyllabics of the laboratory chemists must surely do something for the victim of placebitis.

Porridge

Many forms of food have names unworthy of their flavour. Whatever their merits the titles may be deterrent. Of these unfortunates I would place porridge high on the list. It is a sticky, stodgy word, a repellent label. The Scots can insist that if porridge is made of real oatmeal slowly boiled it has a fine savour and is not at all heavy, but the hours of preparation needed for this treatment are too much for busy people. The Breakfast Cereal type of processed oatmeal was bound to win. The rapidly produced porridge substitute is comparatively cheap, can, but may not, be smooth enough to be palatable, and is certainly filling. Thus stoked goes the child to school, less often the father to his work. Browning never answered his own question about the quality of the porridge provided for John Keats. Probably as a Londoner of his time he was ignorant of this introduction to the trials of the day.

What porridge, we may retort, had Robert Burns? To him it was an evening dish and a principal contributor to *The Cotter's Saturday Night*.

> But now the supper crowns their simple board,
> The halesome parritch chief of Scotia's food.

There was milk, which

> The dame brings forth in complimental mood.

Then to the cheese. Since the English, at least in comic vein, appear to believe that a Scottish meal is unthinkable without haggis, they must be told that there is no mention of that 'Great chieftain o' the puddin-race'.

Any honest Burns-lover will surely admit that, whatever the merits of the halesome dish, this poem shows Burns at his worst. Its closing passage gives the impression of being written after an ill-digested helping of Gray's Elegy. When it ceases to employ Scottish words after the thirteenth stanza and prates in English of the bible-readings, Heaven's Eternal King, the Grace Divine, of simplicity and poverty as 'old Scotia's grandeur' and so on it becomes hard to bear. The praise of whisky on other occasions evoked a genuine zest. *The Cotter's Saturday Night* has all the signs of sanctimonious affectation. I do not believe

103

that Burns enjoyed the austere mixture of 'parritch' and family prayers.

But the Cotter's supper may not have been as suitable to vegetarians as it now is. Porridge is a form of the word pottage, not in itself appetising but less heavy on the lips and in the mouth. Porridge, a word known since 1532, is first explained in the O.E.D. as 'Pottage made by stewing vegetables, herbs, or meat.' Some 'left-overs' from a carnivorous meal did once go into it. So 'Scotia's halesome fare' may have been first cousin to an Irish stew. Wales too may claim to be a participant in the creation of this mess of pottage since *porrum* was the Latin for a leek and porraceous means of 'the nature or colour of the leek'.

Porridge has now been associated with the morning. But Wordsworth as well as Burns thought of it as a supper-time article. He linked the porringer, long a favoured choice for christening presents, with the children's evening

> I take my little porringer
> And eat my supper there.

We Are Seven is not a Wordsworthian example which one chooses to remember. An essay on 'The Influence of Porridge on Poetry' would not be what the learned call encomiastic.

The glutinous syllables are no less a handicap if the first letter is altered. It is hard on a river to be called the Torridge. North Devon has its well-known attractions for the visitor but there is no alluring music in the names of two of its streams whose scenic quality I do not question. A plate of breakfast porridge on the banks of the Taw and the Torridge does not see the palate tingling or bring visions of an enchanting riparian holiday.

Psychedelic

During 1967 psychedelic became a vogue word. It is the nature of vogue words to be vague words; flung about in fashionable chatter they are more confusing than informative. What is in the mind of her who says at a cocktail party 'It's positively psychedelic, my dear'? Probably feelings of delight. But I first heard the word while watching an American television feature about the vagaries and afflictions encountered in a medical hospital. The psychedelic conditions described were induced by hard drugs. Some did seem to indicate a happy 'lift' and even ecstasy in the process of being 'taken for a trip'. But some were terrifying. Evidently the more benignant aspect of psychodelicism has prevailed.

The Penguin English Dictionary of 1965 was brought as far as possible up to date. It does not mention psychedelic. The new Random House Dictionary, an American monster published in Britain by Collins in 1967, includes the word and defines it as 'pertaining to a mental state of great calm' and conveying 'intensely pleasureful perception of the senses'. From that I assume that if I take the right dose of the right dope I shall gain additional pleasure when I listen to music, read poetry, or look at a picture. Perhaps I would be so exalted and certainly I shall not try it. I should, incidentally, be breaking the law and I do not want to be fined or imprisoned for an attempt to improve my faculty of aesthetic appreciation.

Journalism applies the adjective to spectacles from which I gain no 'pleasureful perception' at all. For example I have just seen a photograph of a renowned footballer in the 'big money' class who has had his motor-car, no midget, painted with a fantastic medley of lurid colours. He is described as psychedelic. So is his vehicle. I also read that a similarly bedizened boutique in Baker Street is an essay in psychedelic decoration.

The talker or writer who likes to parade such words as psychedelic is more concerned with mode than meaning in his or her choice of adjectives. What is surprising is the frequent jumble of polysyllabic Hellenism with monosyllabic native slang. We now get psychedelic at one moment and gear the next. A letter from one who long ago left Liverpool for U.S.A. reminds me that gear for smart and striking was Merseyside 'speak' thirty years ago.

Psyche has had a hard time in recent years. She began life as the mortal daughter of an earthly king. Her appearance was so beautiful that she roused the jealousy of the immortal Venus. She also dazzled Cupid. After sundry complications she overcame the envy of Venus. She was then made immortal and united to Cupid for ever. I find no sign in the myth that Psyche ever had lustful thoughts or sinister repressions. She was as innocent as she was lovely, 'a dish' without a stain. What some of the psychoanalysts have done to her is as familiar as it is unfair. The ancient sculptors gave Psyche the wings of a butterfly but she has been turned into the grubbiest of insects by some of our Depth Psychologists whose profundity is not always beyond question.

Psyche has set a puzzle in correct spelling. In the long words of psychotherapeutic medicine the usage prescribes an 'o' in the second syllable. If we write of psycho-analysis and psychoneurosis why not psychodelic?

Q

Quiz

Quizzing has become a major industry in the Britain of today. Opinion Polls, with their tireless pursuit of inquisitive sampling, keep us informed about everything from a Prime Minister's reputation, which still has to be called his image, to our tastes at table and the sexual habits prevalent on a housing estate. A recent discovery of this door-to-door research is that only two per cent of the nation's families eat goose at Christmas. Seventy per cent prefer turkey. How much did it cost to find that out?

Use of the word quiz for an oral examination at school is quite old. The teachers in U.S.A. were quizzing their pupils seventy years ago. Now the television Quiz has become incessant and is obviously popular. The competing school teams have a large public while they undergo and seem to enjoy ordeal by query. In the listing of T.V. favourites *University Challenge* holds, as I write, eleventh place in the Top Twenty. It is as astonishing as it is encouraging that a programme emerging from the dreaming spires and possibly wide-awake quadrangles of modern learning should appear at all on the same map as *Coronation Street, Peyton Place,* and similar thoroughfares of indestructible delight and continuing patronage.

Mention of quiz in the eighteenth century would have indicated a person, not a programme. He was curious, crotchety, and eccentric. If he was a wealthy man with architectural fancies he built himself a Folly. That too could be a quiz. Jane Austen applied the word to a curious article as well as to an odd character. The habitual distrust of abnormal and fantastic taste exposed its owner to the banter and mockery of the average man. So to quiz became a verb for to ridicule. Along with derision went supercilious glances. Hence the name of quizzing-glass for the monocle of the aloof gentleman or the lorgnette raised in disapproval by a frowning milady.

The 'qu' letters are occasionally at the head of agreeable words which demand respect as in queen and quiet. More often they imply doubt and derision. A quirk was a dishonest trick as well as a strange habit. John Galt, whose *Annals of the Parish* provided a rich picture of the Lowland Scots in 1821, wrote of 'a quirkie bodie capable of making law no law at all'.

On the whole, despite the splendour of queens and the possibly seductive charms of the less exalted queans, whose spelling for a young woman has lingered in Broad Scots, the people whose names have this beginning are either unpleasant or odious. The instinct of Dickens was infallible. Quilp must head any list of the horribles. Quack is a good title for a bogus doctor. Contentious pedants are made guilty of quibbles and quiddities. Shakespeare, who may have had an early desk in an attorney's office in his immensely litigious home-town and hated his occupation, added quillets to the catalogue of his detested quirky quibblers. He might have called their cunning queachy since a queach was first a tangle of vegetation and then a contrived confusion of any kind. He liked queasy for distempered. The Roman people were said to be made 'queasy' by Antony's insolence.

The quips of the law were its complications before

quipping became jesting. The quip was often a sarcastic jest since an early meaning of quip and quipping was whip and whipping. Touchstone distinguished between the 'quip modest' and 'reply churlish'. He had not the lash in mind. The flagellant aspect of quipping did not last. But most of the qu's do not invite a smiling reception. I do not want to be met on my door-step by the unfortunate quizzers employed by Opinion Polls and Consumer Research to slog round in all weathers for the satisfaction of public or commercial curiosity. My opinion on the relative values of Butter and Margarine and of rival detergents I prefer to keep to myself. Such queries make me querulous.

R

Rheological

Reading a monthly publication called *Food Manufacture* introduced me to some rather deterrent information about the elaborately 'processed' dietary of our Technological epoch. It also showed that the men engaged in this industry and in writing or reading about it have a vocabulary and an erudition of their own. They carry out most searching tests on their methods and products. This is prudent but reported in baffling form. Are you or any in your company eating ice-cream? Then listen to this. 'Low stress measurements in a co-axial cylinder viscometer at 20° C. simulate the conditions operating on subjective assessment by the palate. Increasing 0.10 per cent fat content increases all measured rheological parameters.' Then it is modestly stated that 'no clear pattern emerges from the data'.

For me no clear pattern of meaning emerges from the lingo. Does 'subjective assessment by the palate' mean anything more than tasting? Viscometer is an instrument for testing glucosity. But the rheological parameters partially defeat my lexicographical research. A parameter is in mathematics 'The third proportional to any given diameter and its conjugate' or, generally, 'a quantity which is constant in a particular case considered but which varies in different cases'. Rheological, apparently a new arrival, presumably refers to moisture since it must be derived from the Greek word for a stream with the inevitable -ology added.

Thus instructed, go to it and enjoy the more that wafer, cornet, or sundae. Sundae I find to be so named because it is 'an ice-cream left over from Sunday and on sale later'. That scarcely increases the attraction. The delay, one fancies, stimulates liquidity or, to use the jargon, adds to the rheological parameters of what you have damply, and I hope deliciously, in hand.

Rumbunctious

When Mr Lee Kuan Yew, the Prime Minister of the City State of Singapore was visiting London to give the British Prime Minister a piece of his mind, he was described before his arrival in the B.B.C.'s *The World at One* programme as rumbunctious. This is not a dictionary word, but its meaning was plain. The Broadcaster did not mean to be impolite. But his use of the adjective could only indicate that Mr Yew was a bustling, ebullient statesman, gusty in temper and violent in the forth-right expression of opinions. When Mr Yew appeared in the *Panorama* programme he turned out to be urbane, good-tempered, shrewd, and a careful chooser of his prudent words. He managed to make a Liberal questioner who blathered about the protective power of the United Nations look foolish and yet did so with calm courtesy. Rumbunctious was the last way in which to picture him.

Other 'rum' words, such as rumbowling and rumbullion which have dictionary status indicate plentiful absorption of grog. But there could be no suggestion that Mr Wilson would have to splice the main-brace lavishly if he were to be a good host. Another 'rummer' is the rumbelow, 'a meaningless combination of syllables, serving as a refrain, originally sung by sailors when rowing'. The first part of the definition recalls what was previously said about flannel and waffle. We have our statesmen who, when all at sea, can do a bit of rumbelowing. But Mr Yew was a model of brevity, precision, and equanimity.

The Scots have rumgumption for good sense with some roughness added. I have had this example of it sent to me. A woman, having to prevent a brawl or 'stramash' among some boys, said 'If I had'na been a wumman of rummagumption the lads would have gillieganted each ither'. My Jamieson's Dictionary of the Scottish Language does not include gillieganting. Its meaning is not hard to guess.

S

Sepulchre

One member of the House of Commons has called
another a whited sepulchre. The discourtesies of that
ill-mannered assembly are many and frequent. To an
ordinary citizen with a code of manners it is astonishing that when the gravest affairs of State are being
discussed the leading speakers on both sides have to
make important statements amid a barrage of what is
vulgarly called chi-iking. The Speaker is constantly
called upon to decide the limits of Parliamentary bad
language. There was some argument and hesitation
about the propriety of using the extremely offensive
sepulchral allusion.

Cruden's *Concordance of the Bible* explains the
words thus. 'It is said that every year on the fifteenth
of February the Jews took care to whiten their sepulchres anew.' Below was the corruption of decaying
flesh. Above the new and cleanly look. Hence the
application to Pharisaical hypocrisy. The member
who used the words could argue that he was quoting
Christ himself. 'Woe unto you, scribes and Pharisees,
hypocrites! For ye are like unto whited sepulchres
which indeed appear beautiful outside, but are within
full of dead men's bones and of all uncleanness'
(Matthew 23, 27). So to give an opponent this name
is at least to compliment him on his good looks whatever the rottenness below.

It has always seemed curious to me that people should talk confidently of 'what Christ said' as though we had verbatim reports immediately recorded on paper. Our Authorised Version of the New Testament is a translation into seventeenth-century English of a Greek version of what Christ was believed to have said in a language called Aramaic defined as 'the northern branch of the Semitic family of languages including Syriac and Chaldee'. He was accompanied by disciples who were not professional reporters and the first texts of the Gospels are generally thought to have been compiled long after, perhaps thirty years after, the events and conversations described. A translation of a translation of a translation does not suggest unchallengeable accuracy. Nor does the time-gap. Speakers in our time are continually complaining that their remarks made yesterday have been misreported or misrepresented by newspapers whose men and women working on jobs of that kind usually have shorthand.

These considerations do not prove that we are greatly misled as to Christ's saying. The most sceptical must admit that his words had powerful effect and were the utterance of an exceptional and commanding personality. When reading was rare the spoken word was more impressive and better remembered than it is now. It is likely that we have the gist of the message as orally handed on by the disciples. A striking metaphor would stamp itself on their attention. The 'whited sepulchre' was part of a trenchant indictment, a pictorial as well as an angry and a stabbing phrase and so could have been vividly and accurately recollected.

Apart from its use in Biblical language our Latin-English sepulchre is a powerful addition to the dark brevity of graves and tombs.

113

> And while our souls negotiate thus
> We like sepulchral statues lay.

The adjective is the bastion of the second line. John Donne wrote thus in *The Ecstasy*. He knew the impact of the word. So of course did Shakespeare when he made Hamlet rhetorically ask

> why the sepulchre
> In which we saw thee quietly inurned
> Hath op'd his ponderous and marble jaws.

If the translators of the New Testament had made Christ call the hypocrites whited graves would his denunciation have been so often quoted? I think not.

Sesquipedalian

Six feet long. Arthur Hugh Clough used the adjective in his poem of epical dimensions *The Bothie of Tober-ma-Vuolich* whose characters are students on a reading party in the Scottish Highlands. That was natural since the poem was written in the English form of the classical six-footed hexameter. He wrote of a 'sesquipedalian blackguard'. Since hexapody is an Anglicised Grecian form of this chosen metre he might have called the fellow a brutish Hexapod.

Sesquipedalians in height have their special utility in the eight forward players of a Rugby football team. When the ball is thrown in from the touch-line the tallest are best equipped to catch it and pass it back to their nimbler back division. Accordingly one possessing sesquipedalian or hexapodic longitude is the target of the thrower-in. To his altitude he adds his powers of leaping for the grab. Some of the most

114

gigantic have been naturally endowed with more inches than the valuable seventy-two. Thus they approach qualification for a further descriptive epithet. We already have such words as septillion for a seventh of a million and a septimole which is a group of seven musical notes. Why not septipedalians on the field of play? If strict accuracy be insisted on quasi-septipedalian could be used. I might recommend it to the Rugby football reporters in whose corps I once occasionally and humbly served. But if that sort of thing was telephoned through to a News Desk I do not think the sub-editors would welcome it. Scholarship has its limits.

Horace introduced *sesquipedalia verba* into his observations on the Art of Poetry. He had a fine talent for writing the quotable and so the adjective was established. One would have expected Ben Jonson, a Latinist from Westminster School and never forgetting it, to have banged this word about the heads of the less erudite in which class he put Shakespeare. In his preface to *Every Man in his Humour* he had a crack at Will who had been accused by the envious Greene of 'bombasting out a blank verse'. If the tradition be true that it was Shakespeare who got Jonson's play accepted after rejection by the Lord Chamberlain's Men the derision was ungenerous. Ben mocked the amplitude of syllables and paucity of stage props in the Shakespearian History Plays. Strangely he did not mention sesquipedalian verbiage but trimmed the length. Shakespeare was accused of making the players 'with three rusty swords' and words of assorted footage 'Fight over York and Lancaster's long Jars'.

The Alchemists of to-day have proliferated feel and syllables as never before in the history of language. Having been notified by my doctor of a salve for acidity of the stomach I read on the directions provided that my 'brand of propantheline bromide' is '2-

diisopropylaminoethylxanthen-9-carboxylate metho-
bromide.' Leaving out the numerals I calculate that
as a twenty-syllabled monster. If that does me no
good words of any length fail me.

Shindig

A shindy with a lot of shouting does not bring to
mind a tolerable kind of noise and to call a party a
shindig, now quite a common practice, does not suggest an addition to gracious living. The makers of
our language seem instinctively to have felt that linking 's' with 'h' is a natural process when liquidity,
especially of a messy kind, is to be described. So we
go splashing and sloshing through a slush, sluice, flush
or wash of waters. Other untidy or repulsive things
have attracted the 'sh' beginning. Shambles is a word
commonly transferred from the gore of the slaughter-
house to signify many kinds of mess and muddle.

There are always exceptions to rules and general-
isations of this kind. Shades and shadows come
musically and atmospherically into many a moving
line of poetry. The words can be spoken without risk
of the hissing and spitting which sibilants can impose.
Good things shine brightly but a reader or reciter of
poetry will not welcome a line which closely unites
the two 'sh' words, the delightful shade and the splashy
shine. Yet Emily Brontë used shine frequently.

> I can see Heaven's glory shine
> And faith shines equal, arming me from fear.

Some poets have managed to include a number of
s's in lines with abiding appeal to the ear. Swinburne
was not at all afraid of that letter. Indeed he was

actually fascinated by it and liked alliteration with this component. 'Oh splendid and sterile Dolores' goes well enough, but I do not find 'the strength of the streams that spring' amenable to the lips. Yet that occurs in the superbly musical summoning and welcome of Spring in the well-known chorus in *Atalanta in Calydon*. Swinburne was lavish with his sibilants, but there is no euphony in 'Stretched out on the spoils that his own hand spread'. Stretch is surely an awkward and ugly word but he did not avoid it. The stretching throats of snakes and other sibilations go together in

> What adders came to shed their coats?
>> What coiled obscene
> Small serpents with soft stretching throats
>> Caressed Faustine?

He did not always keep clear of the slushy sh's.

> Thy lips met with under the status
> Whence a look shot out sharp after theirs.

That is deterrent to one reading aloud. This is to wander from the splash of strong waters which accompany a shindig, a revel at which Swinburne in his untrammelled youth might have surfeited and shone. One so enchanted by showers of salt spray must have used the word shimmering of sunlit waves and waters. P. G. Wodehouse applied it to light movement. 'Jeeves shimmered across the room.' One can see his tactful glide to the rescue if Bertie Wooster was giving a shindig and too lavishly enjoying his own hospitality.

117

Skirmish and Scaramouch

Here is a curious pair of verbal cousins. A skirmish was a pass at fencing before it became a slight, irregular engagement in a war of larger combats. To skiver was an old word for stab or slice. Leather was skived when it was cut into pieces for use in book-binding or the making of garments. Shakespeare's father may have spoken of skiving in his glover's workshop where skins were cut before they were tawed (dressed). His son did not use the term but he wrote of skirmishes in war and of wit in mental conflict. The 'sc' and 'sk' words have been common in the vocabulary of scrap, scrimmage, and the more violent forms of sculduggery.

Skirmish came from a rogue not a tradesman. The dictionaries tell us that skirmish emerged from the world of Scaramouch. In the old Italian farces Scaramuccia made a regular appearance as a liar and poltroon. He was despised and knocked about by Harlequin in the antic skirmishing of the ancient comic ritual. His aged colleague Pantaloon has left us a term for trousers. Scaramouch provided a title of general application for braggarts and scoundrels. Scoundrel too is a descriptive word whose origin is stated to be obscure. To me it suggests a link with skiving and scaramouch characters. Scaramouch passed into the English of contemptuous abuse. Washington Irving used it as an adjective when writing of one who 'swore no scaramouch son of an Italian robber would dare to meddle with an English gentleman'. Have we no scaramouches now among the young vandals and yobs of to-day? It is too good a name to have been forgotten and discarded by those who have a scolding tongue when scamps are abroad. Such frankness is out of date. The scaramouch would now be regarded not as a vicious disturber of the

118

peace but as the disturbed victim of injustice not to be censured for his skirmishing with society.

Snifter

I have been asked why a snifter should be a slang-word for a drink. In that sense it is dated by Eric Partridge at around 1880.

Snifter is not only a slang word. It has been an accepted dictionary word for a strong, rough breeze. Also it has been a cold in the head and a disease of poultry. The idea of hurricane force created the human snifter, a strong, burly, storm-proof fellow. With that, but only in slang, came the strong drink which aided resistance to wind and weather.

There seems to be no use of snifster to describe a captious critic; but the word would fit the type of arbiter in the arts who is always on guard, peering to find a fault, and very fond of the adjectives suspect and disturbing. The kind of writing which many find enjoyable is not going to get past his keen eye and discerning nostril without some dismissive sniffs. Even an alcoholic snifter is not going to warm his heart which contains no heatable cockles. Why those curious cardiac cockles? Perhaps because the heart is shaped like a cockle-shell, perhaps because the marine biologists' name for a cockle is cardium. Whatever the origin of our internal shell-fish, a snifter may raise the human temperature while a snifster has no heart to warm.

Souvenir and Serendipity

In a fascinating article on the acquisitive habits of the Australian bower-bird Mr Alec Chisholm, to whom I owe much useful information on many topics, recorded the astonishing collection of articles amassed by members of this species. Among their oddly assorted booty he included 'silver spoons and jewellery souvenired from rooms with open windows'. Souvenir is a French verb as well as a noun for remembrance and, since we have adopted the noun to describe a keep-sake we might use the Anglicised verb, as he does, for the acquiring process. The tourist industry is now so vast and so productive of souveniring that the memento is in constant demand as the shop-windows prove in all centres of pilgrimage and visitation.

The English on the quest speak of a memo. Keep-sake is a preferable term. Forget-me-not is also simple and sensible, but it is now chiefly the name of a plant, 'the various kinds of Myosotis, chiefly Myosotis Palustris, which has bright blue flowers with a yellow eye'. In the eighteen-twenties there was a fashion for literary souveniring. Volumes of miscellaneous pieces of a gently sentimental kind were published with such titles as Keep-sake and Forget-me-not. I have a reproduction of one, a sweetly sedative form of bed-book worthy of the now fashionable and medical name of tranquilliser.

There was also a volume called *Souvenir* in the continuing series created for the Christmas market by the ingenious Rudolph Ackerman, pioneer in lithography and gifted in many crafts. Other titles of the *Forget-me-Not* annuals were *Bijou, Gem, Amethyst, Winter's Wreath* and *Friendship's Offering*. 'A sound moral lesson' was promised in the choice of contents.

Since these began to appear in 1823 and achieved large sales it is evident that the readers were not all possessed by the cynicism and worldliness of Fourth Georgian London. Victorianism could not have produced anything more daintily elegant and ethical than my *Keep-Sake*. Its illustrations are called embellishments and they earn that prettily genteel description. Embellishing is neither a custom nor a word in use now; a return of the practice might be pleasant. The word is not.

Perhaps a chance copy may be still souvenired in a second-hand book-shop. That would be a case of serendipity, Horace Walpole's word for a lucky find which he invented after reading '*A Tale of Three Princes of Serendip*' (Ceylon) who made happy discoveries of things not expected. There was once a Serendipity Bookshop in Bloomsbury kept by one of the Meynell family. Serendipidist would not be the right name for a bower-bird whose passion for collecting is so indiscriminate. Along with the finery mentioned by Mr Chisholm was a vast assembly of empty cartridge-cases, nails, and scraps of tin!

Spelling Out

Not long ago our statesmen were constantly asked for clarification of their statements. It was a reasonable request for the unwrapping of a parcel of words. It was dignified and courteous; it certainly had not the peremptory ring of the tetchy school-master's 'Explain yourself, fool.' Now, if they are prevailed upon to disclose any hard fact obscured by their verbiage, they are described as spelling out. The phrase crops up whenever I listen to news and comment on the air or read a journalist's political column. 'On Tuesday the Minister will spell out his plans for the readjustment of the grants and allowances necessitated by revaluation.'

At least the spelling out part of such an announcement is welcome to me since I am in the infant class when the Departments of State are drawing up their forms and regulations. I am not as a rule enlightened when the process known as clarification is going on. The clarifiers continue to use the lingo of the Westminster Wafflers and the Tite Barnacles of Whitehall which is variously and impolitely known as Baffle-gab, Gobbledygook, and Barnacular. If only they would indeed become spellers out, monosyllabic and childishly alphabetical. Even should they do so, we might still be baffled. When Mr Weller was asked by the judge about the use of V and W he replied that 'it all depends on the taste and fancy of the speller'. And so it may remain with us when the Minister is asked to 'come clear'.

There is a name, abcdarian, for the devotees of simplicity. I am in this category when about to travel. Bradshaw offers comprehensive schooling but the elementary A.B.C. makes things much easier. The Elizabethan child had his Absey Book, an alphabetical guide to his first groping with the labours of literacy. We have heard a lot about Four Letter Words and we could do with more of them in politics. Our rulers would ease our pains if they could join the spellers out, the abcdarians.

Spliced

It was odd to find spliced used for married by Charlotte Brontë and that not in the jotting of a chatty letter but in the carefully written story of *Villette*. Our customary words for the spliced condition are not beautiful. But they do justice to both the contracting parties since marriage comes from the Latin *maritus,* a husband, while matrimony pays its respects to the intending mother. Spouse is lumpish. Milton used the adjectival form with a fine gravity in his sonnet to his dead wife, 'my late espousèd Saint'. Spouse is more suited to mourning than rejoicing and is not easily grafted onto Hymeneal rites and revels.

When Shakespeare was splicing the four 'happy couples' at the end of *As You Like It* he was evidently tired or bored. Sings Hymen

> 'Peace, ho, I bar confusion.
> 'Tis I must make conclusion
>   Of these most strange events.
> Here's eight that must take hands
> To join in Hymen's bands
>   If truth holds true contents.'

That is so feeble as to indicate derision. The repetition of must is peculiar. Was the poet suggesting that the marriages were tiresomely dutiful and that Free Love would have been more congenial? Apart from any such guess he seems to have been groaning over the heavy contrivance of the fifth act with its sudden unions. Perhaps the leaders of his company were clamouring for a masque to gratify the play-goers who increasingly craved a spectacle. Did the managerial Heminge mutter 'Must have a goddess. They're expected now'? Must again? If he did not like

123

masques he might well respond reluctantly and scribble in the least lyrical of lyrics.

It happened again. Juno comes masquing into *The Tempest* which if not written specially for a wedding was certainly revived for a Court performance when the Princess Elizabeth married the Prince Palatine in 1613. Another must? Juno's benediction on the splicing of Ferdinand and Miranda is perfunctory.

> Honour, riches, marriage blessing,
> Long continuance and increasing,
> Hourly joys be still upon you,
> Juno sings her blessings on you.

The lines are limp and tired. Shakespeare evidently did not care for promenading goddesses and what Bacon called 'the petty wonderments' of the masquing fashion. His genius for the utterance of human love was superb; but the fire went out when there were descents from Olympus.

Our Hymeneal language has not been musical. Byron got most of the vocabulary into four cynical and careless lines in *Don Juan*.

> Romance paints at full length the people's wooings
> But only gives a bust of marriage;
> For no one cares for matrimonial cooings,
> There's nothing wrong with a connubial kiss.
> Think you, if Laura had been Petrarch's wife
> He would have written sonnets all his life?

Connubial is a deterrent word even duller than matrimonial.

Spenser, unlike Shakespeare, could bring an inspired enthusiasm into the greeting of an aristocratic wedding. Both his Prothalamion and Epithalamion Odes are rich in authentic ardour. Nymphs and goddesses did not chill his warmth and evoke doggerel and petty jingling rhymes. He avoided the word marriage and

124

the connubial, matrimonial lingo. He understood that
bride and bridal make music more pleasant to the ear
and bring humanity to Hymeneal raptures.

> Now day is done and night is nighing fast,
> Now bring the Bride into the bridal bowers,
> The night is come and soon her disarray.

And so on to a flowered couch with silken curtains
and 'odoured' sheets. We are a long way from the
frigid 'musts'. Shakespeare had loved his Arden Rosa-
lind and given her his best of glittering lines. But,
with Hymen arriving, he spliced her meagrely.

Spoony

Among the sea-shore Concert Parties of my boyhood
there was talk and sing-song of spooning, which might
lead to splicing. Ballooning was still the only available
form of space-travel and that word, like moon, offered
a convenient rhyme. To take your 'girlie' round the
moon in a balloon was to find the perfect place to
spoon. So ran the 'lyric'. I wondered whether such a
journey was really necessary since spooning of a
modest kind was practised every evening in the
shelters on the Esplanade where the performers had
their open-air stage on a band-stand.

It would be surprising to hear any reference to
spooning now when the pass-the-hat jesters and min-
strels who sang against the noise of wind and wave
have been replaced by the big, well-housed Summer
Show. Even more than flirting spooning is a vanished
word. It has been replaced by dating for necking,
pass-making and (oh, horrible, most horrible) smooch-
ing. The spooners were on their way out when there

was no longer a holiday job for the little tenor who wore a straw-boater and a blazer while he uttered his plaintive love-notes if his company could not run to the pierrot's uniform and the cost of its laundering.

The adjective spoony was used by Thackeray and Trollope. It did not mean flirtatious. The spoony youth was soft and sentimental, not what was later called cissy, but rather one whom we would now talk of as a wet. In Trollope's *The Three Clerks,* early work and far from his best but useful reading for those interested in the curious history of the British Civil Service, Gertrude Woodhouse rejects the courtship of the earnest and severe and even priggish Harry Norman who lets his pushful cousin Alaric Tudor get ahead of him in love at Hampton Court as well as in the bureaucratic rivalry of the Weights and Measures Office. Gertrude says 'There is something spoony in one man allowing another to get before him'. Her mother, the dear, good, correct Mrs Woodhouse, the author's pet, repeats the adjective without censuring her daughter for a vulgarism. With her spoony was not culpably vulgar. There is more talk of Spoonies in this long-winded, sometimes naif, and yet easily readable tale.

That raises the distinction between slang and colloquialism. There would be no slang in the Woodhouse family. To mention a spoony courtier was then to be colloquial but not to be common. Dr Johnson talked of 'colloquial barbarism' but there was nothing outlandish in the conversation imagined by Trollope. Slang, it may be suggested, is the invention of new words or degradation of old ones. Colloquialism is only a slight declension from the completely correct usage. Oxford does not dismiss spoony as slang or even label it colloquial. It began its life early in the nineteenth century as a term for 'foolish, soft, silly'. A quarter of a century later it developed its amorous

126

implications. The careful, shy and hesitant Harry Norman would have been the last person to be aggressively a maker of passes. He was as remote as could be from the sexual wolf of to-day.

Substrate

While seeking news and views of my old University in the December issue of *Oxford,* the biennial publication of the Oxford Society, I read that 'for the wife of the newly appointed Principal of Hertford College long versed, as a physiologist's wife, in irregular hours and impromptu hospitality, the lodgings will provide a new substrate for a familiar skill'. To a Latinist substrate declares its meaning, but being surprised by its appearance in academic housing I turned to Oxford's lexicography for verbal enlightenment. Substrate, I learned, is an anglicised form of Substratum which is a philosophical term for 'that which is regarded as supporting attributes or accidents or that which serves as the basis or foundation of an immaterial thing, condition or activity'. If we turn from metaphysics to substantial things it is an 'under-layer of soil or earthy matter'. A Victorian sociologist wrote of children 'belonging to the substrate of society'.

It is not to be supposed that the Principal of Hertford will earthily entertain in a cavern or a basement and I am confident that the hospitality will be as ample and gracious as if it were practised in what might be called a superstrate. But I am left puzzled by an earlier remark. Why should a renowned Physiologist and his wife be expected to entertain unprepared and at 'irregular hours'. Will the coffee and sandwiches be served or corks be popping in the substrate lodgings at 2 a.m.?

I learned that the Principal had worked most fruitfully with 'back-room boffins' in war-time. Eric Partridge in the Supplement to his *Dictionary of Slang and Unconventional English* tells us that a boffin was heard of before his valuable occupation of posterior premises began in 1939. Why this title? Partridge finds a 'fanciful name of the Lewis Carroll type, yet with a glance at baffle and perhaps at the Boffin Books, a delightful series for children'. He adds that since 1940 it has been in the navy a term for any officer over forty years of age. There seems to be a confusion here with buffer. To return to the curious word with which I began, life at sea has plenty of substrate accommodation if a deck be a stratum.

Sulky

My friend Harold Kynett of Philadelphia, a great lover of the English and Scottish countryside and country towns, has written with accurate knowledge as well as abiding affection of our lands and people. Since his years have diminished the ability, if not the desire, to be in constant and distant motion he has become the devoted historian of Nantucket. There, settling each summer in the island of the old Quaker families and once of the far-wandering whalers, he has found much warmly to love and stoutly to defend against the trend of our pushful times. I do not mention his books under the heading of sulky with the implication that his apprehensions about the survival of the old insular civilization have turned him into a peevish railer. My curiosity was roused by his mention of a Nantucket lady who drives about in a sulky.

Webster's Collegiate Dictionary does suggest that a dislike of company is the origin of that term for 'a little, two-wheeled carriage for a single person'. If it is suitable for single and solitary folk it is conceivable that these persons dislike their fellows. Mr Kynett does not on the whole agree with that. The sulky, he thinks, is not only preferred by people who like solitude as they take a horse (or pony) for a trot along a country road. It is the Vehicle used by a singleton in racing and 'probably derives from the fact that those who failed to win sulked along in this version of what would normally be called a two-wheeled buggy in the United States'. The sulky, as 'a light two-wheeled carriage or chaise, occasionally without a body' has its place in the O.E.D., but the usage is now 'chiefly American'. I take it that the strangely incorporeal conveyance is that of the racing men. There are now so few horses and ponies and fanciers of a jog-trot pace on the road that it is pleasant to hear of one. The English Governess Cart was devised for the outings of that employee of the big country house who took one or more children with her. I suppose it survives. I remember one met in a childhood holiday which was supposed to be propelled by a donkey. Though the load was light he could hardly be coaxed into leaving his home. He indeed was a sulky.

The old carriage-names included the exact opposite of the sulky. The sociable was an open four-wheeled conveyance which had two seats facing each other and a box-seat for the driver. Friendly passengers was the assumption, but there must have been occasional acrimony in the conversation of those sitting confronted in their outing and possibly even what Sir Walter Scott called a tirrivee with sulks to follow.

Swale

Still desolate in our cramped and crowded country is
that northern tip of the North Riding of Yorkshire
which reaches from Swaledale to Teesdale. Here
must be the emptiest wilderness left in England. It
contains at Tan Hill the most elevated and in a hard
winter the least accessible public house in England. The
altitude is 1,834 feet and the nearest inhabited house
is four miles away. Before motor-cars brought visitors
for a drink the inn-keeper could hardly exist on the
thirst of the locals since before then he had no neighbours. He lived mainly by digging up coal which
lay just under the moor. Up to 1914 he sold it at
six shillings a ton; the purchaser had to do his own
cartage.

Swale, probably of Scandinavian origin, is an Old
English word for cold, accurately applied to Tan Hill.
It has also been used of low, wet ground. The banks
of the Swale at the bottom of a precipitous road from
the inn earn its title for both reasons. There is also an
old word Swallet meaning a stream which disappears
underground as many do in the Yorkshire fells. The
pass from the head of Swaledale crossing southwards
into Wensleydale is called Buttertubs because of a
deep hole in the limestone down which one may gaze
to a watery depth. Swalletdale may have been an old
name for the glorious canyon stretching down from
Muker to Yorkshire's Richmond.

However that may be Swale is the right name for
a river that wastes no time. The 'sw' words are a
swirling company, perfectly suited to waters swiftly
swelling after a storm, swooping, swallowing and
swamping the bank-side meadows as they race swill-
ing and swishing on their way.

The people of Swaledale and its over-hanging fells

once mined lead with hard and lethal labour and with small gains as a rule for their risk of lead-poisoning. They had a wonderful sense of words and showed it in their naming of the lonely sheep farms and their delvings in the rock.

The map of the area between Swaledale and Weardale including some of Durham and Westmoreland once turned me into a rhymester; I was not only name-dropping. I had walked past many of these curious titles, known the melancholy of the long deserted mines and seen the relics of old pertinacity where the moor had been tamed by hard hand-labour to yield a meadow on the flank of the scarcely domitable fells. The natives seem to have taken a pleasure in the frank admission of an often cruel climate and of a land that battled to maintain its old freedom of infertility. So I wrote of this wilderness where the air is keen enough to make a man feel born again and where the would-be conquerors of rock and heather injected into their place-names the rough eloquence of their frustration. With my map beside me, I scribbled my rhyme which I hope is not too crude to pass for a kind of rocky poetry. The placenames are all genuine and can, or could be, found on a large-scale map of the wilderness between Swale and Tees.

THE MOORLAND MAP

Our maps are music and our northern titles,
　　Like wind among the grass and heath, grieve.
Our maps are candid charts of desolation
　　And wear the Pennine weather on their sleeve.

There's Howl Moor, Wetshaw, Winterings and
　　　　　　　　　　　　　　　　Gutters,
　　Mirk Fell and Dirty Pool and Hagworm Hill,
Fog Close, Cold Syke, Ravock and Crooks Altar,

And Loups and Wham and Whaw and Rotten
                                    Gill.

Our maps are music and they sing the miners'
    Old wrestle with the rocks for yield of lead :
There's Old Gang, Windegg, Eskeleth, and
                                    Crackpot,
    And Racca Vein, forsaken. They are dead.

Our maps are music and they sing the farmers'
    Long battle to wring fodder from the fell :
There's Stony Mea and Nettlepot and Sour Nook,
    There's Pasture End and Halfpenny, and
                                    Farewell.

Farewell! The perfect name for a sheep-farm which,
if not at 'the back of beyond', is 'yonder' enough to
earn that sad and simple title.

Sybarite

Some cities have had their names perpetuated by
adjectives describing certain characters whose conduct was probably conspicuous but not necessarily
typical. There may have been quite a number of good
family men in Sodom which could not have had a
population without normal parentage. Lot we are
told had a wife.

Labels, earned by a minority, are unjustly adhesive.
No doubt there were abstemious and even austere
men and women in Sybaris when that town became
notorious for its profligate way of life, the earliest
Italian experiment in *dolce vita*.

The English language contains a number of epithets drawn from places and people whom tradition

132

has traduced since the oddities of the few were taken to be the hall-mark of the many. There are the Laodiceans, mentioned in the Book of Revelations and stigmatised for their impassivity and moderation of temper. They would not blow hot or cold; they were a level-headed crowd, proof against rabble-rousers and spell-binding orators, valuable types. But surely there were some enthusiasts about, championing causes or joining Protest Marches. But they have been forgotten and Laodicea's name has lived on to signify placidity in facing the vexed problems of life. Our world is so full of angers, quarrels and wars that the Quietists seem to me to have been setting a good example. But Laodicean has not been a complimentary epithet.

Greece and Asia Minor have provided other place-names which became type-names. By the Elizabethans Ephesus was taken to be a city of friendly frolics and toss-pot revelry. Shakespeare twice wrote of roistering and hospitable folk as Ephesians, both times in Falstaffian episodes. To the English of the nineteenth century Corinth was a symbol of the convivial and sporting life. To be a Corinthian was to be a patron of the cock-pit and the ring. Our Ephesians and Corinthians have gone. The Sybarites have survived two dozen centuries.

Few except classical scholars could explain the origin of the term. Sybaris was an Italian colony founded by Greek merchants in 720 B.C. near the gulf of Tarentum. Their commerce prospered and the successful traders could and did enjoy themselves to the full. They may have been Philistine in Matthew Arnold's sense of the word. (There is another of these labels. The members of that tribe may not all have yawned or shuddered at a work of art.) However that may have been the Sybarites acquired a reputation as the supreme voluptuaries of their age. But

133

their time of self-indulgence was short. Just two hundred years after the gay city was founded it was overrun by the neighbouring Crotonians whose motive, we may assume, was not purely ethical and reformist and whose own habits not grimly austere. It is therefore astonishing that the memory of festive Sybaris should have persisted for nearly two thousand five hundred years. There were some survivors who may have carried on the feasting and revelling in their new city of Thurii. The libertines and debauchees of other ages and other nations were never called Thurians. The later Roman centre of notorious orgies was Capua but we have not called our devotees of luxury and dissipation Capuans. Sybaris perished in its youth and yet retained immortality in the dictionary.

T

Transcendentalism

The Indian sage and yogi have been in the news. So has their devotion to Transcendental Meditation which not long ago made its transitory appeal to the Top-of-the-Poppers, masters of the musical 'beat' and other stars of the entertainment world. It was interesting to learn that they hoped to be fruitfully immersed in philosophic pondering.

Transcendentalism had a lofty origin in the Western

world. To Kant it was a form of thinking 'not derived from experience', to Schelling 'a philosophy of the mind as distinct from that of nature'. In the U.S.A. it was 'the movement of thought in New England of which Emerson was the principal figure'. It also has a most complicated significance in the higher mathematics.

Charles Dickens, when visiting America for the first time in 1842, was baffled by the word then dear to Bostonian intellectuals and wanted to know for what it stood. He met and liked Emerson and his writings which he decided were not only 'fanciful and dreamy but fine and manly, honest and bold'. So he said that, if he became a Bostonian, he would join the Transcendentalists. But one suspects that he did so on the understanding that he would enjoy and share the sturdy manliness and would rather be spared the metaphysics. To Dickens we owe the splendid word 'enthoosimoosy'. Since the original meaning of enthusiasm is 'possession by a god, supernatural inspiration', the devotees of a transcendental religion may accurately be called enthoosimoosiasts.

Transcendental soon lost status as an adjective in a hard and practical world. Benjamin Jowett wrote of 'an unmeaning and transcendental conception'. The snub from Balliol was followed by a general use of the adjective as meaning vague, visionary, and even affected. W. S. Gilbert introduced it in his mockery of the aesthetes in *Patience*. Sang Bunthorne,

'You must lie upon the daisies and discourse in novel
    phrases of your complicated state of mind,
The meaning doesn't matter, if it's only idle chatter
    of a transcendental kind,
        And everyone will say
        As you walk your mystic way,

If this young man expresses himself in terms too
deep for me
Why, why a very singularly deep young man this
deep young man must be.'

The jest is not out of date. As was said in the note
on mystery some of the new mystics are not likely
candidates for triumphant exaltation of the mental
process. Some kind of Enthoosimoosy they may perhaps achieve. One hopes so, but I am left wondering
what those who transcendentally meditate are really
thinking about and what clearly explicable conclu-
sions they reach. They may of course reply that they
just think and think for pure contemplation's sake
and that to ask for results is merely vulgar. For my
part, if I seek the higher summits of abstract thought,
the mind lingers on the foot-hills and these I find to
be soporific. Like the poet Bunthorne I lie on the
daisies, but I make no pretence to his profundity.

As a verb transcend is not to be mocked. It has kept
good company.

'So some strange thoughts transcend our wonted
themes
And into glory peep.

The transcendentalism of Henry Vaughan came long
before Kant and Emerson and evoked poetry of ex-
quisite quality.

V

Villainy

If the B.B.C's once indestructibly genial Dixon of
Dock Green, now quite gruff in manner, and the
ever-welcome Barlow, now less gruff and growling in
his surveillance of westerly Wyvern, are typical of
the real police-station the word villain has ceased to
be theatrical and become the accepted name of their
profession for tough criminals. It is queer to find this
return to what had become the trade-name of old
melodrama's gilded rogues, usually carrying some
such label as Sir Jasper Murgatroyd.

The Jaspers were heavily moustached and blatantly
jewelled as they pursued the heroines with an evil eye
and a sinister, slinky tread. Lyn Harding, a fine actor
of the 'heavies' who later became powerfully classical
in the togas and doublets of Beerbohm Tree's
Shakespearean operations, told me of an old trick
used in his early years of villainy. When his Jaspers
were stalking their prey by night, they had to snarl
'Now all is silence'. A stooge in the audience was engaged to giggle or crack a joke, whereupon Sir Jasper,
replied 'Except for the braying of an ass'. Loud
laughter. The routine never failed. After this retort
villainy went forward to its inevitable frustration by
the Hon Sir Giles Charteris or some such man of
good breeding and unstained virtue.

The up-to-date theatrical progressives talk of

audience-participation in awe-struck tones as though it were something startlingly new. The Victorian villains had it to the full. Henry Mayhew wrote of the screams in the 'Old Vic' gallery when a girl's innocence was threatened. The outcry was not all ethical and cautionary. 'Go to it, my tulip,' was one piece of advice. The 'gods' had their applauders of villainy.

'Villein, one of the serf-class in the feudal system.' He was 'specially a peasant occupier or cultivator entirely subject to a lord'. The latter was the heir to the Roman villa. Milton called a hen 'the villatic fowl'. The human villatics lacked schooling but need not have lacked decency of conduct. That the Middle Ages, idealised by some, had their cruel snobbery is shown by the swift maligning of those now called 'the under-privileged'. It was not long before the villein changed the 'e' for an 'a' and lost his character in the process. Shakespeare's villains are numerous and depraved. They are often regal. The villein working on the land has become the urban cosh-and-grab malefactor of the crime-and-detection world. In the television series the villains are always detected and impounded. Would it were so in fact. The amount of successfully stolen notes in circulation must be enormous and bank-clerks qualify for Danger Money. Shakespeare's 'smiling, damned villain' continues to smile.

W

Wallet

It was nice to see an advertisement of Barclay's Bank in Oxford which sought custom (do Banks have customers or clients?) with the news, made prominent in the caption, that its High Street branch and All Souls College are only 'A Wallet's Throw Apart'. The elasticity of a stone's throw is understood when we read of the distance from the sea advertised in the case of a nearly marine home or home from home. When Bernard Shaw was once stoned by small boys at a time when beards were scarce and was mocked with the cry of 'Beaver' he described his flight from 'lapidation'. There should be a Lapidators' Long Distance Championship open to all house-agents. Bank managers should have a wallet-casting tournament.

When All Souls College was founded a wallet was not what it has come to signify, a repository for paper money, preferably in quantity. In 1546 it was at best a pedlar's pack or at worst the receptacle held out by a beggar. When Shakespeare in his *Troilus and Cressida* made Ulysses observe that Time has a wallet at his back he was thinking of alms not affluence. The O.E.D. does not know the origin of the word, but its new meaning of 'a pocket-book for holding paper money' is attributed to the U.S.A. and dates at 1845. It became an essential in Britain when the sovereigns disappeared in 1914 and has since contained, with luck, more and more paper but, unfortunately, with less and less value. Our financial terms have humble origins. A budget was a pouch or wallet and its ownership was more a sign of the mendicant than the prosperous merchant. A budgeter was a charlatan or strolling player. Budget has grown a capital B and as a national affliction it makes April the cruellest month. It has achieved or suffered a gigantic magnification. If we follow the Barclay use of English we could say that Whitehall is only a Budget's Throw from the Bank of England. Meanwhile Oxonians, whatever their choice of home for an over-draft, will hardly make it by calculating its place in the far-flung Wallet line.

Wander and Wonder

That the partnership of w and r can work powerfully in the words to which they give both power and feeling is shown in wander and wonder. The Wanderer, spelled with a capital, may be the professional member of a football team and working rather than playing for a satisfying reward. But he acquires a pleasant tincture of strangeness from that name and brings a touch of nomadic romance to the towns of Bolton and Wolverhampton whose urban views are not magical. The Wolverhampton team are now generally known as the Wolves and so acquire the status of predators. But wolves are wanderers on their hungry prowl.

Players of games do not wander in isolation in the Wordsworthian manner. The first line of the salute to the Lakeside daffodils, 'I wandered lonely as a cloud', is to me the best in the poem and curiously evocative of a solitude entranced. Cloud itself has a kind of mystery. Shakespeare saw 'far off mountains turned into clouds' and the words, simple as those in 'over the hills and far away', create in themselves a whole landscape of wonder with misty but beckoning peaks. The ghost at Macbeth's banquet with his gory locks shook the haunted host into a string of those monosyllables which Shakespeare could use with shattering effect at the most terrible or pitiful moments.

> 'The time has been
> That, when the brains were out, the man would die
> And there an end, but now they rise again
> With twenty mortal murders on their crowns
> And push us from our stools.'

Except in the fourth line the single syllable suffices. *Macbeth,* with its abundance of murder, is rich in m's and r's and back they come in those astonishing lines

> And overcome us like a summer cloud
> Without our special wonder.

Why in this chamber of horrors are clouds remembered in a summery, not a wintry, sky?

Those who wander in the wilds find wonder there. Wilderness has been a superb invention. Deserts are melancholy places but their name seems mild and trivial if matched with that of a wilderness. 'The waste howling wilderness' is Biblical, occurring in the Book of Deuteronomy. Howling has been the constant adjective for that noun ever since. In the New Testament we are powerfully reminded that wandering can be used in a searing denunciation of the sinful. The Epistle of St. Jude, which is as brief as it is far from bright and brotherly, contains in its scourg-

141

ing prose of the Authorised Version a remarkable roll of the f, r, and w sequence. Those 'giving themselves to fornication and going after strange flesh' are promised the vengeance of eternal fire.

> Woe unto them! for they have gone in the way of Cain, and ran greedily after the error of Balaam for reward, and perished in the gainsaying of Core.
> These are spots in your feasts of charity, when they feast with you, feeding themselves without fear : clouds they are without water, carried about of winds; trees whose fruit withereth, without fruit, twice dead, plucked up by the roots;
> Raging waves of the sea, foaming out their own shame; wandering stars, to whom is reserved the blackness of darkness for ever.

This, when received and duly read, must have made the sinners thus epistolised (that verb is not my invention) wonder what was coming to them.

Wiglomeration

Mr Jarndyce, established in his den which he called the Growlery when the wind was in the east and he was in a mood for making surly noises, denounced with good reason legal delays and obfuscations. He called this tangle Wiglomeration. All his enemies from the Lord Chancellor downwards were wiglomerating round his aching head. It was a term of his own invention. Once there was no such English word as wig; it is a shortening of periwig which is a slurring of *perruque*. The peri was sliced off long ago and wigs have had an extensive life of their own.

142

There are 'wigs on the green' when people quarrel, presumably because these attachments were easily detachable in a brawl. We used to be given a wigging when scolded. But that judicial metaphor is rarely used now. We are told off, given a rocket or put on the carpet. Lately women have taken to wigs on a wide front and sometimes on a lofty scale. The growth of legal wiggery in our time has not ceased. Far from it. I read of a vast new addition in modern 'egg-box' architecture planned to enlarge the now insufficient Gothic pile of the Law Courts. What a theme for Dickens! To this Wiglomeration is added the creative activity of the fashionable hair-dressers. Hair-dressers? Nothing so common. They are all hair-stylists now, and wiglomerating too.

Zap

Here is a nasty newcomer. I first met it in a report of the proceedings in one of the off-off-Broadway theatres where no nastiness is barred. The players and the members of the audience were said to have joined in a love-zap on the stage. Since the definition of rhapsodical quoted on the title-page showed it to be accepted as an adjective for things 'exaggeratedly enthusiastic or ecstatic in manner' the love-zap can be excused inclusion here.

A young American who had just finished his military service told me that zap is a soldiers' word for a violent blow. In Vietnam a man knocked out was said to be zapped. Then I read that a mob of Western students, having discovered a township called Zap, determined to make it the centre of a drink-zap. This became so enthusiastic and ecstatic that they plagued the people of Zap with violent and destructive vandalism. If we are to import the word, the love-zap, however absurd or licentious, is preferable to the hate-zaps favoured by some students in many countries who shout down and menace prominent politicians who have come as the University's guests and then find themselves in a mad-house of slogan shrieking zappery.